MznLnx

Missing Links Exam Preps

Exam Prep for

Mathematics for Elementary Teachers

Musser & Burger & Peterson, 6th Edition

The MznLnx Exam Prep is your link from the texbook and lecture to your exams.
The MznLnx Exam Preps are unauthorized and comprehensive reviews of your textbooks.

All material provided by MznLnx and Rico Publications (c) 2010
Textbook publishers and textbook authors do not particpate in or contribute to these reviews.

MznLnx

Rico
Publications

Exam Prep for Mathematics for Elementary Teachers
6th Edition
Musser & Burger & Peterson

Publisher: Raymond Houge
Assistant Editor: Michael Rouger
Text and Cover Designer: Lisa Buckner
Marketing Manager: Sara Swagger
Project Manager, Editorial Production: Jerry Emerson
Art Director: Vernon Lowerui

Product Manager: Dave Mason
Editorial Assitant: Rachel Guzmanji
Pedagogy: Debra Long
Cover Image: Jim Reed/Getty Images
Text and Cover Printer: City Printing, Inc.
Compositor: Media Mix, Inc.

(c) 2010 Rico Publications

ALL RIGHTS RESERVED. No part of this work covered by the copyright may be reproduced or used in any form or by an means--graphic, electronic, or mechanical, including photocopying, recording, taping, Web distribution, information storage, and retrieval systems, or in any other manner--without the written permission of the publisher.

Printed in the United States
ISBN:

For more information about our products, contact us at:
Dave.Mason@RicoPublications.com

For permission to use material from this text or product, submit a request online to:
Dave.Mason@RicoPublications.com

Contents

CHAPTER 1
INTRODUCTION TO PROBLEM SOLVING — 1

CHAPTER 2
SETS, WHOLE NUMBERS, AND NUMERATION — 8

CHAPTER 3
WHOLE NUMBERS: OPERATIONS AND PROPERTIES — 20

CHAPTER 4
WHOLE-NUMBER COMPUTATION-MENTAL, ELECTRONIC AND WRITTEN — 30

CHAPTER 5
NUMBER THEORY — 39

CHAPTER 6
FRACTIONS — 47

CHAPTER 7
DECIMALS, RATIO, PROPORTION, AND PERCENT — 56

CHAPTER 8
INTEGERS — 64

CHAPTER 9
RATIONAL NUMBERS AND REAL NUMBERS, WITH AN INTRODUCTION TO ALGEBRA — 73

CHAPTER 10
STATISTICS — 86

CHAPTER 11
PROBABILITY — 95

CHAPTER 12
GEOMETRIC SHAPES — 102

CHAPTER 13
MEASUREMENT — 123

CHAPTER 14
GEOMETRY USING TRIANGLE CONGRUENCE AND SIMILARITY — 135

CHAPTER 15
GEOMETRY USING COORDINATES — 146

CHAPTER 16
GEOMETRY USING TRANSFORMATIONS — 151

ANSWER KEY — 165

TO THE STUDENT

COMPREHENSIVE

The *MznLnx* Exam Prep series is designed to help you pass your exams. Editors at MznLnx review your textbooks and then prepare these practice exams to help you master the textbook material. Unlike study guides, workbooks, and practice tests provided by the texbook publisher and textbook authors, *MznLnx* gives you **all** of the material in each chapter in exam form, not just samples, so you can be sure to nail your exam.

MECHANICAL

The MznLnx Exam Prep series creates exams that will help you learn the subject matter as well as test you on your understanding. Each question is designed to help you master the concept. Just working through the exams, you gain an understanding of the subject--its a simple mechanical process that produces success.

INTEGRATED STUDY GUIDE AND REVIEW

MznLnx is not just a set of exams designed to test you, its also a comprehensive review of the subject content. Each exam question is also a review of the concept, making sure that you will get the answer correct without having to go to other sources of material. You learn as you go! Its the easiest way to pass an exam.

HUMOR

Studying can be tedious and dry. MznLnx's instructional design includes moderate humor within the exam questions on occassion, to break the tedium and revitalize the brain

Chapter 1. INTRODUCTION TO PROBLEM SOLVING

1. George Pólya's 1945 book _____ is a small volume describing methods of problem solving.

This book was published at Princeton University. It suggests the following steps when solving a mathematical problem:

1. First, you have to understand the problem.
2. After understanding, then make a plan.
3. Carry out the plan.
4. Look back on your work. How could it be better?

If this technique fails, Pólya advises: 'If you can't solve a problem, then there is an easier problem you can solve: find it.' Or: 'If you cannot solve the proposed problem, try to solve first some related problem. Could you imagine a more accessible related problem?'

His book contains a dictionary-style set of heuristics, many of which have to do with generating a more accessible problem.

- a. The Code Book
- b. How to Solve It
- c. Principia Mathematica
- d. Categories for the Working Mathematician

2. In game theory, a player's _____ in a game is a complete plan of action for whatever situation might arise; this fully determines the player's behaviour. A player's _____ will determine the action the player will take at any stage of the game, for every possible history of play up to that stage.

A _____ profile is a set of strategies for each player which fully specifies all actions in a game.

- a. Matching pennies
- b. Sir Philip Sidney game
- c. Correlated equilibrium
- d. Strategy

3. _____ is a numeral system in which each position is related to the next by a constant multiplier, a common ratio, called the base or radix of that numeral system.
- a. NegaFibonacci coding
- b. Cyrillic numerals
- c. Negative base
- d. Place Value

4. The _____ are the set of numbers consisting of the natural numbers including 0 and their negatives. They are numbers that can be written without a fractional or decimal component, and fall within the set {... −2, −1, 0, 1, 2, ...}.
- a. A Mathematical Theory of Communication
- b. Integers
- c. A posteriori
- d. A chemical equation

5. Exponentiation is a mathematical operation, written a^n, involving two numbers, the base a and the _____ n. When n is a positive integer, exponentiation corresponds to repeated multiplication:

$$a^n = \underbrace{a \times \cdots \times a}_{n},$$

just as multiplication by a positive integer corresponds to repeated addition:

$$a \times n = \underbrace{a + \cdots + a}_{n}.$$

The _____ is usually shown as a superscript to the right of the base. The exponentiation a^n can be read as: a raised to the n-th power, a raised to the power [of] n or possibly a raised to the _____ [of] n, or more briefly: a to the n-th power or a to the power [of] n, or even more briefly: a to the n.

    a. Exponential sum   b. Exponentiating by squaring
    c. Exponential tree   d. Exponent

6. In mathematics, computing, linguistics and related subjects, an _____ is a sequence of finite instructions, often used for calculation and data processing. It is formally a type of effective method in which a list of well-defined instructions for completing a task will, when given an initial state, proceed through a well-defined series of successive states, eventually terminating in an end-state. The transition from one state to the next is not necessarily deterministic; some _____s, known as probabilistic _____s, incorporate randomness.

    a. Out-of-core   b. Approximate counting algorithm
    c. In-place algorithm   d. Algorithm

7. In cryptography, _____ is a pseudorandom number generator and a stream cipher designed by Robert Jenkins to be cryptographically secure. The name is an acronym for Indirection, Shift, Accumulate, Add, and Count.

The _____ algorithm has similarities with RC4.

    a. Order   b. Imputation
    c. Isaac   d. Introduction

8. The _____ (symbol: N) is the SI derived unit of force, named after Isaac _____ in recognition of his work on classical mechanics.

The _____ is the unit of force derived in the SI system; it is equal to the amount of force required to accelerate a mass of one kilogram at a rate of one meter per second per second. Algebraically:

$$1\text{ N} = 1\ \frac{\text{kg} \cdot \text{m}}{\text{s}^2}.$$

- 1 N is the force of Earth's gravity on an object with a mass of about 102 g ($^1\!/_{9.8}$ kg) (such as a small apple.)
- On Earth's surface, a mass of 1 kg exerts a force of approximately 9.80665 N [down] (or 1 kgf.) The approximation of 1 kg corresponding to 10 N is sometimes used as a rule of thumb in everyday life and in engineering.
- The force of Earth's gravity on a human being with a mass of 70 kg is approximately 687 N.
- The dot product of force and distance is mechanical work. Thus, in SI units, a force of 1 N exerted over a distance of 1 m is 1 NÂ·m of work. The Work-Energy Theorem states that the work done on a body is equal to the change in energy of the body. 1 NÂ·m = 1 J (joule), the SI unit of energy.
- It is common to see forces expressed in kilonewtons or kN, where 1 kN = 1 000 N.

a. 120-cell
b. Newton
c. 2-3 heap
d. 1-center problem

9. In World War II, _____ was the United States codename for intelligence derived from the cryptanalysis of PURPLE, a Japanese foreign office cipher.

The Japanese and the Germans both used the Enigma machine to encode their cable traffic. The Japanese Enigma-based system was called PURPLE by U.S. cryptographers.

a. Basis
b. Magic
c. Bandwidth
d. Discontinuity

10. In recreational mathematics, a _____ of order n is an arrangement of n^2 numbers, usually distinct integers, in a square, such that the n numbers in all rows, all columns, and both diagonals sum to the same constant. A normal _____ contains the integers from 1 to n^2. The term '_____' is also sometimes used to refer to any of various types of word square.

a. 120-cell
b. 1-center problem
c. Prime reciprocal magic square
d. Magic square

11. In probability theory and statistics the _____ in favour of an event or a proposition are the quantity p /, where p is the probability of the event or proposition. The _____ against the same event are / p. For example, if you chose a random day of the week, then the _____ that you would choose a Sunday would be 1/6, not 1/7.

a. Event
b. Estimation of covariance matrices
c. Anscombe transform
d. Odds

12. A _____, from the French patron, is a type of theme of recurring events of or objects, sometimes referred to as elements of a set. These elements repeat in a predictable manner. It can be a template or model which can be used to generate things or parts of a thing, especially if the things that are created have enough in common for the underlying _____ to be inferred, in which case the things are said to exhibit the unique _____.

a. 2-3 heap
b. 1-center problem
c. 120-cell
d. Pattern

13. Leonardo of Pisa (c. 1170 - c. 1250), also known as Leonardo Pisano, Leonardo Bonacci, Leonardo _____, or, most commonly, simply _____, was an Italian mathematician, considered by some 'the most talented mathematician of the Middle Ages'.
a. Harry Hinsley
b. Guido Castelnuovo
c. Ralph C. Merkle
d. Fibonacci

14. Induction or _____, sometimes called inductive logic, is the process of reasoning in which the premises of an argument are believed to support the conclusion but do not entail it;. Induction is a form of reasoning that makes generalizations based on individual instances. It is used to ascribe properties or relations to types based on an observation instance; or to formulate laws based on limited observations of recurring phenomenal patterns.
a. Intuitionistic logic
b. Affine logic
c. Idempotency of entailment
d. Inductive reasoning

15. In mathematics, a _____, sometimes also called a perfect square, is an integer that can be written as the square of some other integer; in other words, it is the product of some integer with itself. So, for example, 9 is a _____, since it can be written as 3 × 3. _____s are non-negative.
a. Hexagonal number
b. Pentagonal pyramidal number
c. Centered pentagonal number
d. Square number

16. In mathematics, a _____ can mean either an element of the set {1, 2, 3, ...} or an element of the set {0, 1, 2, 3, ...}. The latter is especially preferred in mathematical logic, set theory, and computer science.

_____s have two main purposes: they can be used for counting, and they can be used for ordering.

a. Cardinal numbers
b. Strong partition cardinal
c. Suslin cardinal
d. Natural number

17. A _____ is one of the basic shapes of geometry: a polygon with three corners or vertices and three sides or edges which are line segments. A _____ with vertices A, B, and C is denoted ABC.

In Euclidean geometry any three non-collinear points determine a unique _____ and a unique plane.

a. Fuhrmann circle
b. 1-center problem
c. Kepler triangle
d. Triangle

18. In mathematics, the _____ of a number n is the number that, when added to n, yields zero. The _____ of n is denoted −n. For example, 7 is −7, because 7 + (−7) = 0, and the _____ of −0.3 is 0.3, because −0.3 + 0.3 = 0.
a. Algebraic structure
b. Associativity
c. Arity
d. Additive inverse

19. The _____ or Towers of Hanoi is a mathematical game or puzzle. It consists of three rods, and a number of disks of different sizes which can slide onto any rod. The puzzle starts with the disks neatly stacked in order of size on one rod, the smallest at the top, thus making a conical shape.

Chapter 1. INTRODUCTION TO PROBLEM SOLVING

a. 2-3 heap
c. 1-center problem
b. 120-cell
d. Tower of Hanoi

20.

_____ is a Unicode block of 96 symbols at hex codepoint range 25A0-25FF. This range contains various _____.

Only two font sets--Code2000 and the DejaVu family--include coverage for each of the glyphs in the _____ range.

a. 1-center problem
c. Geometric shapes
b. 120-cell
d. 2-3 heap

21. The _____ of an object located in some space refers to the part of space occupied by the object as determined by its external boundary -- abstracting from other aspects the object may have such as its colour, content as well as from the object's position and orientation in space, and its size.

According to famous mathematician and statistician David George Kendall, _____ may be defined as

Simple two-dimensional _____s can be described by basic geometry such as points, line, curves, plane, and so on. _____s that occur in the physical world are often quite complex; they may be arbitrarily curved as studied by differential geometry as for plants or coastlines.)

a. Spidron
c. Parallel lines
b. Confocal
d. Shape

22. A _____ is the sum of the n natural numbers from 1 to n.

$$T_n = 1 + 2 + 3 + \cdots + (n-1) + n = \frac{n(n+1)}{2} = \frac{n^2+n}{2} \stackrel{\text{def}}{=} \binom{n+1}{2}$$

As shown in the rightmost term of this formula, every _____ is a binomial coefficient: the nth triangular is the number of distinct pairs to be selected from n + 1 objects. In this form it solves the 'handshake problem' of counting the number of handshakes if each person in a room full of n+1 total people shakes hands once with each other person.

a. Heptagonal number
c. Centered pentagonal number
b. Star number
d. Triangular number

23. In mathematics, a _____ is a picture of a straight line in which the integers are shown as specially-marked points evenly spaced on the line. Although this image only shows the integers from -9 to 9, the line includes all real numbers, continuing 'forever' in each direction. It is often used as an aid in teaching simple addition and subtraction, especially involving negative numbers.

Chapter 1. INTRODUCTION TO PROBLEM SOLVING

    a. Number system
    b. Point plotting
    c. Real number
    d. Number Line

24. The _____ is a mathematical curve and one of the earliest fractal curves to have been described. It appeared in a 1904 paper titled 'On a continuous curve without tangents, constructible from elementary geometry' by the Swedish mathematician Helge von Koch. The lesser known _____ is the same as the snowflake, except it starts with a line segment instead of an equilateral triangle.

    a. Continuous linear extension
    b. Biscuspid
    c. Control flow graph
    d. Koch curve

25. The _____ is a mathematical curve and one of the earliest fractal curves to have been described. It appeared in a 1904 paper entitled "On a continuous curve without tangents constructible from elementary geometry" by the Swedish mathematician Helge von Koch.

    a. 1-center problem
    b. 2-3 heap
    c. 120-cell
    d. Koch snowflake

26. In mathematics, the concept of a _____ tries to capture the intuitive idea of a geometrical one-dimensional and continuous object. A simple example is the circle. In everyday use of the term '_____', a straight line is not curved, but in mathematical parlance _____s include straight lines and line segments.

    a. Negative pedal curve
    b. Quadrifolium
    c. Curve
    d. Kappa curve

27. A _____ is a figurate number that extends the concept of triangular and square numbers to the pentagon, but, unlike the first two, the patterns involved in the construction of _____s are not rotationally symmetrical. The nth _____ p_n is the number of distinct dots in a pattern of dots consisting of the outlines of regular pentagons whose sides contain 1 to n dots, overlaid so that they share one vertex. For instance, the third one is formed from outlines comprising 1, 5 and 10 dots, but the 1, and 3 of the 5, coincide with 3 of the 10 - leaving 12 distinct dots, 10 in the form of a pentagon, and 2 inside...

    a. Critical line theorem
    b. Holonomic constant
    c. Multiplicative partition
    d. Pentagonal number

28. In computer science an _____ is a data structure consisting of a group of elements that are accessed by indexing. In most programming languages each element has the same data type and the _____ occupies a contiguous area of storage.

Most programming languages have a built-in _____ data type, although what is called an _____ in the language documentation is sometimes really an associative _____.

    a. A posteriori
    b. A chemical equation
    c. Array
    d. A Mathematical Theory of Communication

29. _____ is the mathematical operation of scaling one number by another. It is one of the four basic operations in elementary arithmetic.

_____ is defined for whole numbers in terms of repeated addition; for example, 4 multiplied by 3 can be calculated by adding 3 copies of 4 together:

$$4 + 4 + 4 = 12.$$

_____ of rational numbers and real numbers is defined by systematic generalization of this basic idea.

a. The number 0 is even.
c. Highest common factor
b. Least common multiple
d. Multiplication

Chapter 2. SETS, WHOLE NUMBERS, AND NUMERATION

1. Wikipedia has thousands of topic lists; some are even lists of other lists

    _____ - By belief - By nationality - By occupation - By office held - By prize won

    a. George Glauberman
    c. Kenneth Kunen
    b. People
    d. William Hugh Woodin

2. A _____ is a 2D geometric symbolic representation of information according to some visualization technique. Sometimes, the technique uses a 3D visualization which is then projected onto the 2D surface. The word graph is sometimes used as a synonym for _____.
    a. 2-3 heap
    c. 120-cell
    b. 1-center problem
    d. Diagram

3. In game theory, a player's _____ in a game is a complete plan of action for whatever situation might arise; this fully determines the player's behaviour. A player's _____ will determine the action the player will take at any stage of the game, for every possible history of play up to that stage.

    A _____ profile is a set of strategies for each player which fully specifies all actions in a game.

    a. Matching pennies
    c. Sir Philip Sidney game
    b. Correlated equilibrium
    d. Strategy

4. In mathematics, the _____ is a direct product of sets. The _____ is named after René Descartes, whose formulation of analytic geometry gave rise to this concept.

    Specifically, the _____ of two sets X and Y, denoted X × Y, is the set of all possible ordered pairs whose first component is a member of X and whose second component is a member of Y:

    $$X \times Y = \{(x,y) | x \in X \text{ and } y \in Y\}.$$

    For example, the _____ of the 13-element set of standard playing card ranks {Ace, King, Queen, Jack, 10, 9, 8, 7, 6, 5, 4, 3, 2} and the four-element set of card suits {â™ , â™¥, â™¦, â™£} is the 52-element set of all possible playing cards ,, ...,, ...,}.

    a. Choice function
    c. Set of all sets
    b. Disjoint sets
    d. Cartesian product

5. In mathematics, an _____ or member of a set is any one of the distinct objects that make up that set.

    Writing A = {1,2,3,4}, means that the _____s of the set A are the numbers 1, 2, 3 and 4. Groups of _____s of A, for example {1,2}, are subsets of A.

    a. Element
    c. Ideal
    b. Universal code
    d. Order

Chapter 2. SETS, WHOLE NUMBERS, AND NUMERATION

6. In mathematics, and more specifically set theory, the _____ is the unique set having no members. Some axiomatic set theories assure that the _____ exists by including an axiom of _____; in other theories, its existence can be deduced. Many possible properties of sets are trivially true for the _____.
   a. A Mathematical Theory of Communication
   b. Inverse function
   c. Empty set
   d. Empty function

7. In the study of metric spaces in mathematics, there are various notions of two metrics on the same underlying space being 'the same', or _____.

In the following, M will denote a non-empty set and d_1 and d_2 will denote two metrics on M.

The two metrics d_1 and d_2 are said to be topologically _____ if they generate the same topology on M.

   a. A chemical equation
   b. A Mathematical Theory of Communication
   c. A posteriori
   d. Equivalent

8. In mathematics, a _____ can mean either an element of the set {1, 2, 3, ...} or an element of the set {0, 1, 2, 3, ...}. The latter is especially preferred in mathematical logic, set theory, and computer science.

_____s have two main purposes: they can be used for counting, and they can be used for ordering.

   a. Suslin cardinal
   b. Strong partition cardinal
   c. Natural number
   d. Cardinal numbers

9. In mathematics, a _____ is a set that is negligible in some sense. For different applications, the meaning of 'negligible' varies. In measure theory, any set of measure 0 is called a _____.
   a. Prevalence and shyness
   b. Borel-Cantelli lemma
   c. Radonifying function
   d. Null set

10. _____ or set diagrams are diagrams that show all hypothetically possible logical relations between a finite collection of sets. _____ were invented around 1880 by John Venn. They are used in many fields, including set theory, probability, logic, statistics, and computer science.
   a. 2-3 heap
   b. 120-cell
   c. 1-center problem
   d. Venn diagrams

11. In mathematics, a _____ can mean either an element of the set {1, 2, 3, ...} (i.e the positive integers) or an element of the set {0, 1, 2, 3, ...} (i.e. the non-negative integers).
   a. Degrees of freedom
   b. Whole number
   c. FISH
   d. Bounded

12. In a positional numeral system, the decimal separator is a symbol used to mark the boundary between the integral and the fractional parts of a decimal numeral. When used in context of Arabic numerals, terms implying the symbol used are _____ and decimal comma.

The decimal separator is mathematically a radix point.

a. Tetradecimal
b. Hexadecimal
c. Fibonacci coding
d. Decimal point

13. In geometry, a _____ is a part of a line that is bounded by two distinct end points, and contains every point on the line between its end points. Examples of _____s include the sides of a triangle or square. More generally, when the end points are both vertices of a polygon, the _____ is either an edge if they are adjacent vertices, or otherwise a diagonal.
   a. Golden angle
   b. Transversal line
   c. Cuboid
   d. Line segment

14. In mathematics, two sets are said to be disjoint if they have no element in common. For example, {1, 2, 3} and {4, 5, 6} are _____.

Formally, two sets A and B are disjoint if their intersection is the empty set.
wikimedia.org/math/b/3/5/b35d3befc06b831ff4d6cd63bf922efb.png">

This definition extends to any collection of sets.

   a. Subset
   b. Horizontal line test
   c. Preimage
   d. Disjoint sets

15. In the mathematical discipline of graph theory a _____ or edge independent set in a graph is a set of edges without common vertices. It may also be an entire graph consisting of edges without common vertices.

Given a graph G =, a _____ M in G is a set of pairwise non-adjacent edges; that is, no two edges share a common vertex.

   a. Route inspection problem
   b. Cut vertex
   c. Road coloring theorem
   d. Matching

16. In mathematics, especially in set theory, a set A is a _____ of a set B if A is 'contained' inside B. Notice that A and B may coincide. The relationship of one set being a _____ of another is called inclusion.
   a. Horizontal line test
   b. Subset
   c. Cartesian product
   d. Set of all sets

17. In mathematics, and particularly in applications to set theory and the foundations of mathematics, a _____ or universal class is a class that contains all of the elements and sets that one may wish to use in a given situation. There are several versions of this general idea, described in the following sections.

Perhaps the simplest version is that any set can be a _____, so long as the object of study is confined to that particular set.

   a. Universe
   b. Operation
   c. A chemical equation
   d. A Mathematical Theory of Communication

Chapter 2. SETS, WHOLE NUMBERS, AND NUMERATION

18. In mathematics and computer science, _____ (also base-16, hexa or base, of 16. It uses sixteen distinct symbols, most often the symbols 0-9 to represent values zero to nine, and A, B, C, D, E, F (or a through f) to represent values ten to fifteen.

Its primary use is as a human friendly representation of binary coded values, so it is often used in digital electronics and computer engineering.

   a. Tetradecimal
   b. Radix
   c. Factoradic
   d. Hexadecimal

19. A _____ is one of the basic shapes of geometry: a polygon with three corners or vertices and three sides or edges which are line segments. A _____ with vertices A, B, and C is denoted ABC.

In Euclidean geometry any three non-collinear points determine a unique _____ and a unique plane.

   a. 1-center problem
   b. Kepler triangle
   c. Triangle
   d. Fuhrmann circle

20. In mathematics, the _____ of two sets A and B is the set that contains all elements of A that also belong to B, but no other elements.

For explanation of the symbols used in this article, refer to the table of mathematical symbols.

The _____ of A and B

The _____ of A and B is written 'A ∩ B'. Formally:

   x is an element of A ∩ B if and only if
   - x is an element of A and
   - x is an element of B.
   For example:
   - The _____ of the sets {1, 2, 3} and {2, 3, 4} is {2, 3}.
   - The number 9 is not in the _____ of the set of prime numbers {2, 3, 5, 7, 11, â€¦} and the set of odd numbers {1, 3, 5, 7, 9, 11, â€¦}.

If the _____ of two sets A and B is empty, that is they have no elements in common, then they are said to be disjoint, denoted: A ∩ B = ∅. For example the sets {1, 2} and {3, 4} are disjoint, written {1, 2} ∩ {3, 4} = ∅.

   a. Erlang
   b. Advice
   c. Order
   d. Intersection

Chapter 2. SETS, WHOLE NUMBERS, AND NUMERATION

21. In set theory, the term _____ refers to a set operation used in the convergence of set elements to form a resultant set containing the elements of both sets. As a simple example, a _____ of two disjoint sets, which do not have elements in common results in a set containing all elements from both sets. A Venn diagram representing the _____ of sets A and B.
   a. Introduction
   b. Event
   c. UES
   d. Union

22. In geometry and trigonometry, an _____ is the figure formed by two rays sharing a common endpoint, called the vertex of the _____. The magnitude of the _____ is the 'amount of rotation' that separates the two rays, and can be measured by considering the length of circular arc swept out when one ray is rotated about the vertex to coincide with the other. Where there is no possibility of confusion, the term '_____' is used interchangeably for both the geometric configuration itself and for its angular magnitude.
   a. A posteriori
   b. A chemical equation
   c. A Mathematical Theory of Communication
   d. Angle

23. In discrete mathematics and predominantly in set theory, a _____ is a concept used in comparisons of sets to refer to the unique values of one set in relation to another. The terms 'absolute' and 'relative' _____ refer to more specific applications of the concept, with universal _____s referring to elements unique to the universal set and the latter referring to the unique elements of one set in relation to another. In this image, the universal set is represented by the border of the image, and the set A as a disc.
   a. Complement
   b. Derivative algebra
   c. Huge
   d. Kernel

24.
_____ is a Unicode block of 96 symbols at hex codepoint range 25A0-25FF. This range contains various _____.

Only two font sets--Code2000 and the DejaVu family--include coverage for each of the glyphs in the _____ range.

   a. 120-cell
   b. 2-3 heap
   c. 1-center problem
   d. Geometric shapes

25. In probability theory, an _____ is a set of outcomes to which a probability is assigned. Typically, when the sample space is finite, any subset of the sample space is an _____. However, this approach does not work well in cases where the sample space is infinite, most notably when the outcome is a real number.
   a. Audio compression
   b. Information set
   c. Event
   d. Equaliser

26. The _____ of an object located in some space refers to the part of space occupied by the object as determined by its external boundary -- abstracting from other aspects the object may have such as its colour, content as well as from the object's position and orientation in space, and its size.

According to famous mathematician and statistician David George Kendall, _____ may be defined as

Chapter 2. SETS, WHOLE NUMBERS, AND NUMERATION

Simple two-dimensional _____s can be described by basic geometry such as points, line, curves, plane, and so on. _____s that occur in the physical world are often quite complex; they may be arbitrarily curved as studied by differential geometry as for plants or coastlines.)

   a. Shape   b. Parallel lines
   c. Spidron   d. Confocal

27. In quantum field theory and statistical mechanics in the thermodynamic limit, a system with a global symmetry can have more than one phase. For parameters where the symmetry is spontaneously broken, the system is said to be _____. When the global symmetry is unbroken the system is disordered.
   a. Ursell function   b. Isoenthalpic-isobaric ensemble
   c. Ordered   d. Einstein relation

28. In mathematics, an _____ is a collection of objects having two coordinates (or entries or projections), such that one can always uniquely determine the object, which is the first coordinate (or first entry or left projection) of the pair as well as the second coordinate (or second entry or right projection.) If the first coordinate is a and the second is b, the usual notation for an _____ is (a, b.) The pair is 'ordered' in that (a, b) differs from (b, a) unless a = b.
   a. A chemical equation   b. A Mathematical Theory of Communication
   c. Ordered pair   d. A posteriori

29. In mathematics, _____ are generalized numbers used to measure the cardinality of sets. For finite sets, the cardinality is given by a natural number, which is simply the number of elements in the set. There are also transfinite _____ that describe the sizes of infinite sets.
   a. Strong partition cardinal   b. Cardinal numbers
   c. Cardinality of the continuum   d. Suslin cardinal

30. In mathematics, an _____ in the sense of ring theory is a subring $\mathcal{O}$ of a ring R that satisfies the conditions

1. R is a ring which is a finite-dimensional algebra over the rational number field $\mathbb{Q}$
2. $\mathcal{O}$ spans R over $\mathbb{Q}$, so that $\mathbb{Q}\mathcal{O} = R$, and
3. $\mathcal{O}$ is a lattice in R.

The third condition can be stated more accurately, in terms of the extension of scalars of R to the real numbers, embedding R in a real vector space. In less formal terms, additively $\mathcal{O}$ should be a free abelian group generated by a basis for R over $\mathbb{Q}$.

The leading example is the case where R is a number field K and $\mathcal{O}$ is its ring of integers. In algebraic number theory there are examples for any K other than the rational field of proper subrings of the ring of integers that are also _____s.

14 *Chapter 2. SETS, WHOLE NUMBERS, AND NUMERATION*

    a. Annihilator   b. Efficiency
    c. Algebraic   d. Order

31. In mathematics, an inequality is a statement about the relative size or order of two objects. For example 14 > 10, or 14 is _____ 10. The notation a > b means that a is _____ b and 'a' would be to the right of 'b' on a number line.
    a. Cauchy-Schwarz inequality   b. Greater than
    c. FKG inequality   d. Minkowski inequality

32. In mathematics, a _____ is a picture of a straight line in which the integers are shown as specially-marked points evenly spaced on the line. Although this image only shows the integers from -9 to 9, the line includes all real numbers, continuing 'forever' in each direction. It is often used as an aid in teaching simple addition and subtraction, especially involving negative numbers.
    a. Number system   b. Number line
    c. Point plotting   d. Real number

33. In mathematics, _____ and undefined are used to explain whether or not expressions have meaningful, sensible, and unambiguous values. Not all branches of mathematics come to the same conclusion.

The following expressions are undefined in all contexts, but remarks in the analysis section may apply.

    a. Defined   b. LHS
    c. Toy model   d. Plugging in

34. _____ is a numeral system in which each position is related to the next by a constant multiplier, a common ratio, called the base or radix of that numeral system.
    a. Negative base   b. NegaFibonacci coding
    c. Cyrillic numerals   d. Place value

35. In mathematics, the term _____ has several different important meanings:

- An _____ is an equality that remains true regardless of the values of any variables that appear within it, to distinguish it from an equality which is true under more particular conditions. For this, the 'triple bar' symbol ≡ is sometimes used.
- In algebra, an _____ or _____ element of a set S with a binary operation Â· is an element e that, when combined with any element x of S, produces that same x. That is, eÂ·x = xÂ·e = x for all x in S.
  - The _____ function from a set S to itself, often denoted id or id_S, s the function such that i = x for all x in S. This function serves as the _____ element in the set of all functions from S to itself with respect to function composition.
  - In linear algebra, the _____ matrix of size n is the n-by-n square matrix with ones on the main diagonal and zeros elsewhere. This matrix serves as the _____ with respect to matrix multiplication.

A common example of the first meaning is the trigonometric _____

$$\sin^2 \theta + \cos^2 \theta = 1$$

which is true for all real values of θ, as opposed to

$$\cos\theta = 1,$$

which is true only for some values of θ, not all. For example, the latter equation is true when $\theta = 0$, false when $\theta = 2$

The concepts of 'additive _____' and 'multiplicative _____' are central to the Peano axioms. The number 0 is the 'additive _____' for integers, real numbers, and complex numbers. For the real numbers, for all $a \in \mathbb{R}$,

$$0 + a = a,$$

$$a + 0 = a, \text{ and}$$

$$0 + 0 = 0.$$

Similarly, The number 1 is the 'multiplicative _____' for integers, real numbers, and complex numbers.

a. Identity
b. ARIA
c. Action
d. Intersection

36. In ecology, predation describes a biological interaction where a _____ (an organism that is hunting) feeds on its prey, the organism that is attacked. _____s may or may not kill their prey prior to feeding on them, but the act of predation always results in the death of the prey. The other main category of consumption is detritivory, the consumption of dead organic material (detritus.)
a. 1-center problem
b. 120-cell
c. Prey
d. Predator

37. In mathematics, the _____ is a term used to describe the number of times one must apply a given operation to an integer before reaching a fixed point.

Usually, this refers to the additive or multiplicative persistence of an integer, which is how often one has to replace the number by the sum or product of its digits until one reaches a single digit. Because the numbers are broken down into their digits, the additive or multiplicative persistence depends on the radix.

a. Linear congruence theorem
b. Lychrel number
c. Coprime
d. Persistence of a number

Chapter 2. SETS, WHOLE NUMBERS, AND NUMERATION

38. In mathematics, the _____ is an approach to finding a particular solution to certain inhomogeneous ordinary differential equations and recurrence relations. It is closely related to the annihilator method, but instead of using a particular kind of differential operator in order to find the best possible form of the particular solution, a 'guess' is made as to the appropriate form, which is then tested by differentiating the resulting equation. In this sense, the _____ is less formal but more intuitive than the annihilator method.

   a. Phase line
   b. Differential algebraic equations
   c. Linear differential equation
   d. Method of undetermined coefficients

39. An _____ is a calculating tool used primarily in parts of Asia for performing arithmetic processes. Today, abaci are often constructed as a bamboo frame with beads sliding on wires, but originally they were beans or stones moved in grooves in sand or on tablets of wood, stone, or metal. The _____ was in use centuries before the adoption of the written modern numeral system and is still widely used by merchants, traders and clerks in Asia, Japan, Africa, India and elsewhere.

   a. A posteriori
   b. A chemical equation
   c. A Mathematical Theory of Communication
   d. Abacus

40. _____ is simply the manner of writing out an expression in full. When a quantity is written as a sum of terms, or as a continued product, _____ notation is used to illustrate the expression in its entirety.

   a. Algebra
   b. Algebraic function
   c. Algebraic element
   d. Expanded form

41. Exponentiation is a mathematical operation, written a^n, involving two numbers, the base a and the _____ n. When n is a positive integer, exponentiation corresponds to repeated multiplication:

$$a^n = \underbrace{a \times \cdots \times a}_{n},$$

just as multiplication by a positive integer corresponds to repeated addition:

$$a \times n = \underbrace{a + \cdots + a}_{n}.$$

The _____ is usually shown as a superscript to the right of the base. The exponentiation a^n can be read as: a raised to the n-th power, a raised to the power [of] n or possibly a raised to the _____ [of] n, or more briefly: a to the n-th power or a to the power [of] n, or even more briefly: a to the n.

   a. Exponential tree
   b. Exponential sum
   c. Exponentiating by squaring
   d. Exponent

42. In functional analysis, a Banach space is called _____ if it satisfies a certain abstract property involving dual spaces. _____ spaces turn out to have desirable geometric properties.

Suppose X is a normed vector space over R or C.

Chapter 2. SETS, WHOLE NUMBERS, AND NUMERATION

a. Gamma test
b. Copula
c. Boolean algebra
d. Reflexive

43. _____ is the likelihood or chance that something is the case or will happen. Theoretical _____ is used extensively in areas such as statistics, mathematics, science and philosophy to draw conclusions about the likelihood of potential events and the underlying mechanics of complex systems.

The word _____ does not have a consistent direct definition.

a. Standardized moment
b. Probability
c. Discrete random variable
d. Statistical significance

44. In mathematics, an _____ is a binary relation between two elements of a set which groups them together as being 'equivalent' in some way. Let a, b, and c be arbitrary elements of some set X. Then 'a ~ b' or 'a ≡ b' denotes that a is equivalent to b.

a. A chemical equation
b. Equivalence relation
c. Equivalence class
d. A Mathematical Theory of Communication

45. The mathematical concept of a _____ expresses the intuitive idea of deterministic dependence between two quantities, one of which is viewed as primary and the other as secondary. A _____ then is a way to associate a unique output for each input of a specified type, for example, a real number or an element of a given set.

a. Function
b. Coherent
c. Grill
d. Going up

46. In number theory, a _____ of a positive integer n is a way of writing n as a sum of positive integers. Two sums which only differ in the order of their summands are considered to be the same _____; if order matters then the sum becomes a composition. A summand in a _____ is also called a part.

a. Derivative algebra
b. Distribution
c. Congruent
d. Partition

47. In mathematics, a _____ X is a division of X into non-overlapping 'parts' or 'blocks' or 'cells' that cover all of X. More formally, these 'cells' are both collectively exhaustive and mutually exclusive with respect to the set being partitioned.

A _____ X is a set of nonempty subsets of X such that every element x in X is in exactly one of these subsets.

a. Cycle index
b. Partition of a set
c. Set packing
d. Block walking

48. In mathematics, a binary relation R over a set X is transitive if whenever an element a is related to an element b, and b is in turn related to an element c, then a is also related to c.

Transitivity is a key property of both partial order relations and equivalence relations.

For example, 'is greater than,' 'is at least as great as,' and 'is equal to' are _____s:

whenever A > B and B > C, then also A > C
whenever A ≥ B and B ≥ C, then also A ≥ C
whenever A = B and B = C, then also A = C

For some time, economists and philosophers believed that preference was a _____ however there are now mathematical theories which demonstrate that preferences and other significant economic results can be modelled without resorting to this assumption.

a. Totally ordered set
c. Directed set
b. Partial function
d. Transitive Relation

49. In mathematics, an arithmetic progression or _____ is a sequence of numbers such that the difference of any two successive members of the sequence is a constant. For instance, the sequence 3, 5, 7, 9, 11, 13... is an arithmetic progression with common difference 2.

a. Alternating series test
c. Edgeworth series
b. Eisenstein series
d. Arithmetic sequence

50. The x-axis is the horizontal axis of a two- dimensional plot in the _____, that is typically pointed to the right. Also known as a right-handed coordinate system.

a. 2-3 heap
c. 1-center problem
b. Cartesian coordinate system
d. 120-cell

51. Leonardo of Pisa (c. 1170 - c. 1250), also known as Leonardo Pisano, Leonardo Bonacci, Leonardo _____, or, most commonly, simply _____, was an Italian mathematician, considered by some 'the most talented mathematician of the Middle Ages'.

a. Guido Castelnuovo
c. Fibonacci
b. Harry Hinsley
d. Ralph C. Merkle

52. Initial objects are also called _____, and terminal objects are also called final.

a. Colimit
c. Direct limit
b. Terminal object
d. Coterminal

53. The _____ is a function in mathematics. The application of this function to a value x is written as ex. Equivalently, this can be written in the form e^x, where e is a mathematical constant, the base of the natural logarithm, which equals approximately 2.718281828, and is also known as Euler's number.

a. A chemical equation
c. Exponential function
b. A Mathematical Theory of Communication
d. Area hyperbolic functions

54. In computer science an _____ is a data structure consisting of a group of elements that are accessed by indexing. In most programming languages each element has the same data type and the _____ occupies a contiguous area of storage.

Chapter 2. SETS, WHOLE NUMBERS, AND NUMERATION   19

Most programming languages have a built-in _____ data type, although what is called an _____ in the language documentation is sometimes really an associative _____.

a. A posteriori
b. A chemical equation
c. A Mathematical Theory of Communication
d. Array

55. _____ occurs when the growth rate of a mathematical function is proportional to the function's current value. In the case of a discrete domain of definition with equal intervals it is also called geometric growth or geometric decay.

With _____ of a positive value its rate of increase steadily increases, or in the case of exponential decay, its rate of decrease steadily decreases.

a. A chemical equation
b. A posteriori
c. A Mathematical Theory of Communication
d. Exponential growth

56. In mathematics, especially in the area of abstract algebra known as ring theory, a _____ is a ring with 0 ≠ 1 such that ab = 0 implies that either a = 0 or b = 0. That is, it is a nontrivial ring without left or right zero divisors. A commutative _____ is called an integral _____.

a. Modular representation theory
b. Simple ring
c. Left primitive ring
d. Domain

57. In descriptive statistics, the _____ is the length of the smallest interval which contains all the data. It is calculated by subtracting the smallest observations from the greatest and provides an indication of statistical dispersion.

It is measured in the same units as the data.

a. Kernel
b. Class
c. Bandwidth
d. Range

58. In mathematics and in the sciences, a _____ (plural: _____e, formulæ or _____s) is a concise way of expressing information symbolically (as in a mathematical or chemical _____), or a general relationship between quantities. One of many famous _____e is Albert Einstein's $E = mc^2$ (see special relativity

In mathematics, a _____ is a key to solve an equation with variables. For example, the problem of determining the volume of a sphere is one that requires a significant amount of integral calculus to solve.

a. 120-cell
b. 1-center problem
c. Formula
d. 2-3 heap

Chapter 3. WHOLE NUMBERS: OPERATIONS AND PROPERTIES

1. An _____ is a calculating tool used primarily in parts of Asia for performing arithmetic processes. Today, abaci are often constructed as a bamboo frame with beads sliding on wires, but originally they were beans or stones moved in grooves in sand or on tablets of wood, stone, or metal. The _____ was in use centuries before the adoption of the written modern numeral system and is still widely used by merchants, traders and clerks in Asia, Japan, Africa, India and elsewhere.
   a. A Mathematical Theory of Communication
   b. A chemical equation
   c. A posteriori
   d. Abacus

2. In mathematics, a _____ can mean either an element of the set {1, 2, 3, ...} (i.e the positive integers) or an element of the set {0, 1, 2, 3, ...} (i.e. the non-negative integers).
   a. FISH
   b. Bounded
   c. Whole number
   d. Degrees of freedom

3. In game theory, a player's _____ in a game is a complete plan of action for whatever situation might arise; this fully determines the player's behaviour. A player's _____ will determine the action the player will take at any stage of the game, for every possible history of play up to that stage.

   A _____ profile is a set of strategies for each player which fully specifies all actions in a game.

   a. Strategy
   b. Matching pennies
   c. Sir Philip Sidney game
   d. Correlated equilibrium

4. In mathematics, the _____ is a direct product of sets. The _____ is named after René Descartes, whose formulation of analytic geometry gave rise to this concept.

   Specifically, the _____ of two sets X and Y, denoted X × Y, is the set of all possible ordered pairs whose first component is a member of X and whose second component is a member of Y:

   $$X \times Y = \{(x,y) | x \in X \text{ and } y \in Y\}.$$

   For example, the _____ of the 13-element set of standard playing card ranks {Ace, King, Queen, Jack, 10, 9, 8, 7, 6, 5, 4, 3, 2} and the four-element set of card suits {♠, ♥, ♦, ♣} is the 52-element set of all possible playing cards ,, ...,,, ...,,}.

   a. Disjoint sets
   b. Set of all sets
   c. Choice function
   d. Cartesian product

5. In ecology, predation describes a biological interaction where a _____ (an organism that is hunting) feeds on its prey, the organism that is attacked. _____s may or may not kill their prey prior to feeding on them, but the act of predation always results in the death of the prey. The other main category of consumption is detritivory, the consumption of dead organic material (detritus.)
   a. 120-cell
   b. 1-center problem
   c. Predator
   d. Prey

6. An _____ is a number which is involved in addition. A number being added is considered to be an _____.

Chapter 3. WHOLE NUMBERS: OPERATIONS AND PROPERTIES 21

a. Addend
b. A chemical equation
c. A posteriori
d. A Mathematical Theory of Communication

7. _____ is the likelihood or chance that something is the case or will happen. Theoretical _____ is used extensively in areas such as statistics, mathematics, science and philosophy to draw conclusions about the likelihood of potential events and the underlying mechanics of complex systems.

The word _____ does not have a consistent direct definition.

a. Discrete random variable
b. Statistical significance
c. Standardized moment
d. Probability

8. In mathematics, computing, linguistics and related subjects, an _____ is a sequence of finite instructions, often used for calculation and data processing. It is formally a type of effective method in which a list of well-defined instructions for completing a task will, when given an initial state, proceed through a well-defined series of successive states, eventually terminating in an end-state. The transition from one state to the next is not necessarily deterministic; some _____s, known as probabilistic _____s, incorporate randomness.

a. Algorithm
b. Approximate counting algorithm
c. In-place algorithm
d. Out-of-core

9. In mathematics, a _____ is a calculation involving two operands, in other words, an operation whose arity is two. _____s can be accomplished using either a binary function or binary operator. _____s are sometimes called dyadic operations in order to avoid confusion with the binary numeral system.

a. 1-center problem
b. 2-3 heap
c. 120-cell
d. Binary operation

10. In mathematics and computer science, _____ (also base-16, hexa or base, of 16. It uses sixteen distinct symbols, most often the symbols 0-9 to represent values zero to nine, and A, B, C, D, E, F (or a through f) to represent values ten to fifteen.

Its primary use is as a human friendly representation of binary coded values, so it is often used in digital electronics and computer engineering.

a. Radix
b. Tetradecimal
c. Factoradic
d. Hexadecimal

11. The framework of quantum mechanics requires a careful definition of _____, and a thorough discussion of its practical and philosophical implications.

_____ is viewed in different ways in the many interpretations of quantum mechanics; however, despite the considerable philosophical differences, they almost universally agree on the practical question of what results from a routine quantum-physics laboratory _____. To describe this, a simple framework to use is the Copenhagen interpretation, and it will be implicitly used in this section; the utility of this approach has been verified countless times, and all other interpretations are necessarily constructed so as to give the same quantitative predictions as this in almost every case.

a. Fundamental units
b. Dynamic range
c. 1-center problem
d. Measurement

12. In mathematics, a _____ is a picture of a straight line in which the integers are shown as specially-marked points evenly spaced on the line. Although this image only shows the integers from -9 to 9, the line includes all real numbers, continuing 'forever' in each direction. It is often used as an aid in teaching simple addition and subtraction, especially involving negative numbers.

  a. Number system
  b. Point plotting
  c. Number line
  d. Real number

13. In mathematics, a set is said to be _____ if the operation on members of the set produces a member of the set. For example, the real numbers are closed under subtraction, but the natural numbers are not: 3 and 7 are both natural numbers, but the result of 3 − 7 is not.

Similarly, a set is said to be closed under a collection of operations if it is closed under each of the operations individually.

  a. Contingency table
  b. Control chart
  c. Closed under some operation
  d. Continuous linear extension

14. The _____ is a rule which states that when you add or multiply numbers, changing the order doesn't change the result.

  a. Commutative law
  b. Semigroupoid
  c. Conditional event algebra
  d. Coimage

15. In mathematics the _____ of a set which is equipped with the operation of addition is an element which, when added to any element x in the set, yields x. One of the most familiar additive identities is the number 0 from elementary mathematics, but additive identities occur in other mathematical structures where addition is defined, such as in groups and rings.

- The _____ familiar from elementary mathematics is zero, denoted 0. For example,

    5 + 0 = 5 = 0 + 5.

- In the natural numbers N and all of its supersets, the _____ is 0. Thus for any one of these numbers n,

    n + 0 = n = 0 + n.

Let N be a set which is closed under the operation of addition, denoted +. An _____ for N is any element e such that for any element n in N,

    e + n = n = n + e.

  a. Unique factorization domain
  b. Additive identity
  c. Unit ring
  d. Algebraically independent

Chapter 3. WHOLE NUMBERS: OPERATIONS AND PROPERTIES

16. In mathematics, the term _____ has several different important meanings:

- An _____ is an equality that remains true regardless of the values of any variables that appear within it, to distinguish it from an equality which is true under more particular conditions. For this, the 'triple bar' symbol ≡ is sometimes used.
- In algebra, an _____ or _____ element of a set S with a binary operation Â· is an element e that, when combined with any element x of S, produces that same x. That is, eÂ·x = xÂ·e = x for all x in S.
  - The _____ function from a set S to itself, often denoted id or id_S, s the function such that i = x for all x in S. This function serves as the _____ element in the set of all functions from S to itself with respect to function composition.
  - In linear algebra, the _____ matrix of size n is the n-by-n square matrix with ones on the main diagonal and zeros elsewhere. This matrix serves as the _____ with respect to matrix multiplication.

A common example of the first meaning is the trigonometric _____

$$\sin^2\theta + \cos^2\theta = 1$$

which is true for all real values of θ, as opposed to

$$\cos\theta = 1,$$

which is true only for some values of θ, not all. For example, the latter equation is true when $\theta = 0$, false when $\theta = 2$

The concepts of 'additive _____' and 'multiplicative _____' are central to the Peano axioms. The number 0 is the 'additive _____' for integers, real numbers, and complex numbers. For the real numbers, for all $a \in \mathbb{R}$,

$$0 + a = a,$$

$a + 0 = a$, and

$$0 + 0 = 0.$$

Similarly, The number 1 is the 'multiplicative _____' for integers, real numbers, and complex numbers.

a. Identity
c. Action
b. Intersection
d. ARIA

17. In mathematics, _____ is a property that a binary operation can have. It means that, within an expression containing two or more of the same associative operators in a row, the order that the operations are performed does not matter as long as the sequence of the operands is not changed. That is, rearranging the parentheses in such an expression will not change its value.

Chapter 3. WHOLE NUMBERS: OPERATIONS AND PROPERTIES

a. Associativity
b. Algebraically closed
c. Unital
d. Idempotence

18. In combinatorial mathematics, a _____ is an un-ordered collection of distinct elements, usually of a prescribed size and taken from a given set. Given such a set S, a _____ of elements of S is just a subset of S, where as always forsets the order of the elements is not taken into account. Also, as always forsets, no elements can be repeated more than once in a _____; this is often referred to as a 'collection without repetition'.

a. Sparsity
b. Heawood number
c. Combination
d. Fill-in

19. In discrete mathematics and predominantly in set theory, a _____ is a concept used in comparisons of sets to refer to the unique values of one set in relation to another. The terms 'absolute' and 'relative' _____ refer to more specific applications of the concept, with universal _____s referring to elements unique to the universal set and the latter referring to the unique elements of one set in relation to another. In this image, the universal set is represented by the border of the image, and the set A as a disc.

a. Complement
b. Huge
c. Derivative algebra
d. Kernel

20. In mathematics, an _____ or member of a set is any one of the distinct objects that make up that set.

Writing A = {1,2,3,4}, means that the _____s of the set A are the numbers 1, 2, 3 and 4. Groups of _____s of A, for example {1,2}, are subsets of A.

a. Order
b. Universal code
c. Ideal
d. Element

21. The traditional names for the parts of the formula c − b = a, are _____ (c) − subtrahend (b) = difference (a). The words _____ and subtrahend are uncommon in modern usage. Instead we say that c and −b are terms, and treat subtraction as addition of the opposite. The answer is still called the difference.

a. Multiplication
b. Plus and minus signs
c. Lowest common denominator
d. Minuend

22. The quantity that is deducted from the minuend in subtraction is the _____.

a. Subtrahend
b. Trailing zeros
c. The number 0 is even.
d. Lowest common denominator

23. A _____ is a word, phrase, number or other sequence of units that can be read the same way in either direction. Composing literature in _____s is an example of constrained writing. The word '_____' was coined from Greek roots palin and dromos by English writer Ben Jonson in the 1600s.

a. Metalanguage
b. 120-cell
c. 1-center problem
d. Palindrome

24. In mathematics, the notion of cancellative is a generalization of the notion of invertible.

An element a in a magma has the left _____ if for all b and c in M, a * b = a * c always implies b = c.

Chapter 3. WHOLE NUMBERS: OPERATIONS AND PROPERTIES

An element a in a magma has the right _____ if for all b and c in M, b * a = c * a always implies b = c.

   a. Magmas that are commutative but not associative
   b. Cancellation property
   c. Quasifield
   d. Power associativity

25. The _____ are the set of numbers consisting of the natural numbers including 0 and their negatives. They are numbers that can be written without a fractional or decimal component, and fall within the set {... −2, −1, 0, 1, 2, ...}.
   a. A posteriori
   b. A chemical equation
   c. A Mathematical Theory of Communication
   d. Integers

26. _____ is the mathematical operation of scaling one number by another. It is one of the four basic operations in elementary arithmetic.

_____ is defined for whole numbers in terms of repeated addition; for example, 4 multiplied by 3 can be calculated by adding 3 copies of 4 together:

$$4 + 4 + 4 = 12.$$

_____ of rational numbers and real numbers is defined by systematic generalization of this basic idea.

   a. Highest common factor
   b. The number 0 is even.
   c. Least common multiple
   d. Multiplication

27. In computer science an _____ is a data structure consisting of a group of elements that are accessed by indexing. In most programming languages each element has the same data type and the _____ occupies a contiguous area of storage.

Most programming languages have a built-in _____ data type, although what is called an _____ in the language documentation is sometimes really an associative _____.

   a. A chemical equation
   b. A Mathematical Theory of Communication
   c. A posteriori
   d. Array

28. In statistics, the _____
   a. Factorial code
   b. Confirmatory factor analysis
   c. Scatter matrix
   d. Generalized linear array model

29. A _____ is an algorithm to multiply two numbers. Depending on the size of the numbers, different algorithms are in use. Efficient _____s have been around since the advent of the decimal system.
   a. Spigot algorithm
   b. Double dabble
   c. Karatsuba algorithm
   d. Multiplication algorithm

30. A _____ is a 2D geometric symbolic representation of information according to some visualization technique. Sometimes, the technique uses a 3D visualization which is then projected onto the 2D surface. The word graph is sometimes used as a synonym for _____.

Chapter 3. WHOLE NUMBERS: OPERATIONS AND PROPERTIES

a. 1-center problem
b. 120-cell
c. 2-3 heap
d. Diagram

31. In set theory, a _____ is a partially ordered set such that for each t ∈ T, the set {s ∈ T : s < t} is well-ordered by the relation <. For each t ∈ T, the order type of {s ∈ T : s < t} is called the height of t. The height of T itself is the least ordinal greater than the height of each element of T.

a. Transitive reduction
b. Set-theoretic topology
c. Definable numbers
d. Tree

32. In mathematics, and in particular in abstract algebra, distributivity is a property of binary operations that generalises the _____ law from elementary algebra.

a. Permutation
b. Closure with a twist
c. General linear group
d. Distributive

33. _____s are payments made by a corporation to its shareholder members. When a corporation earns a profit or surplus, that money can be put to two uses: it can either be re-invested in the business, or it can be paid to the shareholders as a _____. Many corporations retain a portion of their earnings and pay the remainder as a _____.

a. Dividend
b. 120-cell
c. 1-center problem
d. GNU Privacy Guard

34. In mathematics, a _____ of an integer n is an integer which evenly divides n without leaving a remainder. For example, 7 is a _____ of 42 because 42/7 = 6. We also say 42 is divisible by 7 or 42 is a multiple of 7 or 7 divides 42 or 7 is a factor of 42 and we usually write 7 | 42.

a. 1-center problem
b. 120-cell
c. Divisor
d. 2-3 heap

35. In mathematics, a _____ is the end result of a division problem. It can also be expressed as the number of times the divisor divides into the dividend.

a. Quotient
b. Marginal cost
c. Notation
d. Limiting

36. In mathematics, a division is called a _____ if the divisor is zero. Such a division can be formally expressed as $\frac{a}{0}$ where a is the dividend. Whether this expression can be assigned a well-defined value depends upon the mathematical setting.

a. 120-cell
b. 1-center problem
c. 2-3 heap
d. Division by Zero

37. Exponentiation is a mathematical operation, written a^n, involving two numbers, the base a and the _____ n. When n is a positive integer, exponentiation corresponds to repeated multiplication:

$$a^n = \underbrace{a \times \cdots \times a}_{n},$$

Chapter 3. WHOLE NUMBERS: OPERATIONS AND PROPERTIES   27

just as multiplication by a positive integer corresponds to repeated addition:

$$a \times n = \underbrace{a + \cdots + a}_{n}.$$

The _____ is usually shown as a superscript to the right of the base. The exponentiation a^n can be read as: a raised to the n-th power, a raised to the power [of] n or possibly a raised to the _____ [of] n, or more briefly: a to the n-th power or a to the power [of] n, or even more briefly: a to the n.

- a. Exponential sum
- b. Exponential tree
- c. Exponentiating by squaring
- d. Exponent

38. In mathematics, an _____ in the sense of ring theory is a subring $\mathcal{O}$ of a ring R that satisfies the conditions

  1. R is a ring which is a finite-dimensional algebra over the rational number field $\mathbb{Q}$
  2. $\mathcal{O}$ spans R over $\mathbb{Q}$, so that $\mathbb{Q}\mathcal{O} = R$, and
  3. $\mathcal{O}$ is a lattice in R.

The third condition can be stated more accurately, in terms of the extension of scalars of R to the real numbers, embedding R in a real vector space. In less formal terms, additively $\mathcal{O}$ should be a free abelian group generated by a basis for R over $\mathbb{Q}$.

The leading example is the case where R is a number field K and $\mathcal{O}$ is its ring of integers. In algebraic number theory there are examples for any K other than the rational field of proper subrings of the ring of integers that are also _____s.

- a. Annihilator
- b. Efficiency
- c. Order
- d. Algebraic

39. In mathematics, an inequality is a statement about the relative size or order of two objects. For example 14 > 10, or 14 is _____ 10. The notation a > b means that a is _____ b and 'a' would be to the right of 'b' on a number line.

- a. Greater than
- b. Cauchy-Schwarz inequality
- c. FKG inequality
- d. Minkowski inequality

40. In mathematics, a _____ is a statement that can be proved on the basis of explicitly stated or previously agreed assumptions.

- a. Boolean function
- b. Disjunction introduction
- c. Logical value
- d. Theorem

41. A _____, from the French patron, is a type of theme of recurring events of or objects, sometimes referred to as elements of a set. These elements repeat in a predictable manner. It can be a template or model which can be used to generate things or parts of a thing, especially if the things that are created have enough in common for the underlying _____ to be inferred, in which case the things are said to exhibit the unique _____.

a. 120-cell
b. 1-center problem
c. 2-3 heap
d. Pattern

42. _____ was a Hungarian American mathematician who made major contributions to a vast range of fields, including set theory, functional analysis, quantum mechanics, ergodic theory, continuous geometry, economics and game theory, computer science, numerical analysis, hydrodynamics, and statistics, as well as many other mathematical fields. He is generally regarded as one of the foremost mathematicians of the 20th century. The mathematician Jean Dieudonné called von Neumann 'the last of the great mathematicians.' Most notably, von Neumann was a pioneer of the application of operator theory to quantum mechanics, a principal member of the Manhattan Project and the Institute for Advanced Study in Princeton, and a key figure in the development of game theory and the concepts of cellular automata and the universal constructor.

a. John von Neumann
b. Stuart Milner-Barry
c. Frederick William Winterbotham
d. Hemachandra Surä«

43. In mathematics, an _____ is a statement about the relative size or order of two objects, or about whether they are the same or not

- The notation a < b means that a is less than b.
- The notation a > b means that a is greater than b.
- The notation a ≠ b means that a is not equal to b, but does not say that one is bigger than the other or even that they can be compared in size.

In all these cases, a is not equal to b, hence, '_____'.

These relations are known as strict _____

- The notation a ≤ b means that a is less than or equal to b;
- The notation a ≥ b means that a is greater than or equal to b;

An additional use of the notation is to show that one quantity is much greater than another, normally by several orders of magnitude.

- The notation a << b means that a is much less than b.
- The notation a >> b means that a is much greater than b.

If the sense of the _____ is the same for all values of the variables for which its members are defined, then the _____ is called an 'absolute' or 'unconditional' _____. If the sense of an _____ holds only for certain values of the variables involved, but is reversed or destroyed for other values of the variables, it is called a conditional _____.

An _____ may appear unsolvable because it only states whether a number is larger or smaller than another number; but it is possible to apply the same operations for equalities to inequalities. For example, to find x for the _____ 10x > 23 one would divide 23 by 10.

a. A Mathematical Theory of Communication b. A chemical equation
c. A posteriori d. Inequality

Chapter 4. WHOLE-NUMBER COMPUTATION-MENTAL, ELECTRONIC AND WRITTEN

1. An _____ is a calculating tool used primarily in parts of Asia for performing arithmetic processes. Today, abaci are often constructed as a bamboo frame with beads sliding on wires, but originally they were beans or stones moved in grooves in sand or on tablets of wood, stone, or metal. The _____ was in use centuries before the adoption of the written modern numeral system and is still widely used by merchants, traders and clerks in Asia, Japan, Africa, India and elsewhere.

   a. A posteriori
   b. A Mathematical Theory of Communication
   c. A chemical equation
   d. Abacus

2. The _____ was an automatic, mechanical calculator designed to tabulate polynomial functions. Both logarithmic and trigonometric functions can be approximated by polynomials, so a _____ can compute many useful sets of numbers. Closeup of the London Science Museum's _____. Per Georg Scheutz's third _____

   J. H. Müller, an engineer in the Hessian army conceived the idea in a book published in 1786, but failed to find funding to progress this further.

   a. 120-cell
   b. Difference Engine
   c. 1-center problem
   d. 2-3 heap

3. In mathematics, especially in geometry and group theory, a _____ in R^n is a discrete subgroup of R^n which spans the real vector space R^n. Every _____ in R^n can be generated from a basis for the vector space by forming all linear combinations with integral coefficients. A _____ may be viewed as a regular tiling of a space by a primitive cell.

   a. Homogeneity
   b. Boundary
   c. Group
   d. Lattice

4. _____ was a German polymath who wrote primarily in Latin and French.

   He occupies an equally grand place in both the history of philosophy and the history of mathematics. He invented infinitesimal calculus independently of Newton, and his notation is the one in general use since then.

   a. Harry Hinsley
   b. Michel Rolle
   c. Raymond Merrill Smullyan
   d. Gottfried Wilhelm Leibniz

5. In mathematics, the _____ of a number to a given base is the power or exponent to which the base must be raised in order to produce the number.

   For example, the _____ of 1000 to the base 10 is 3, because 3 is how many 10s one must multiply to get 1000: thus 10 × 10 × 10 = 1000; the base-2 _____ of 32 is 5 because 5 is how many 2s one must multiply to get 32: thus 2 × 2 × 2 × 2 × 2 = 32. In the language of exponents: 10^3 = 1000, so $\log_{10} 1000 = 3$, and $2^5 = 32$, so $\log_2 32 = 5$.

   a. 1-center problem
   b. 2-3 heap
   c. 120-cell
   d. Logarithm

6. The _____ is a mechanical analog computer. The _____ is used primarily for multiplication and division, and also for 'scientific' functions such as roots, logarithms and trigonometry, but does not generally perform addition or subtraction.

Chapter 4. WHOLE-NUMBER COMPUTATION-MENTAL, ELECTRONIC AND WRITTEN 31

_____s come in a diverse range of styles and generally appear in a linear or circular form with a standardized set of markings essential to performing mathematical computations.

a. 2-3 heap
c. Slide rule
b. 1-center problem
d. 120-cell

7. An _____ is a type of calculator, usually specialized for bookkeeping calculations. In the United States, the earliest _____s were usually built to read in dollars and cents. _____s were ubiquitous office equipment until they were phased out in favor of personal computers, beginning in about 1985.
a. A posteriori
c. A Mathematical Theory of Communication
b. A chemical equation
d. Adding machine

8. In game theory, a player's _____ in a game is a complete plan of action for whatever situation might arise; this fully determines the player's behaviour. A player's _____ will determine the action the player will take at any stage of the game, for every possible history of play up to that stage.

A _____ profile is a set of strategies for each player which fully specifies all actions in a game.

a. Sir Philip Sidney game
c. Matching pennies
b. Correlated equilibrium
d. Strategy

9. In mathematics, the _____ is a direct product of sets. The _____ is named after René Descartes, whose formulation of analytic geometry gave rise to this concept.

Specifically, the _____ of two sets X and Y, denoted X × Y, is the set of all possible ordered pairs whose first component is a member of X and whose second component is a member of Y:

$$X \times Y = \{(x,y) | x \in X \text{ and } y \in Y\}.$$

For example, the _____ of the 13-element set of standard playing card ranks {Ace, King, Queen, Jack, 10, 9, 8, 7, 6, 5, 4, 3, 2} and the four-element set of card suits {â™ , â™¥, â™¦, â™£} is the 52-element set of all possible playing cards ,, ...,,, ...,}.

a. Choice function
c. Disjoint sets
b. Set of all sets
d. Cartesian product

10. In mathematics, computing, linguistics and related subjects, an _____ is a sequence of finite instructions, often used for calculation and data processing. It is formally a type of effective method in which a list of well-defined instructions for completing a task will, when given an initial state, proceed through a well-defined series of successive states, eventually terminating in an end-state. The transition from one state to the next is not necessarily deterministic; some _____s, known as probabilistic _____s, incorporate randomness.
a. In-place algorithm
c. Algorithm
b. Out-of-core
d. Approximate counting algorithm

Chapter 4. WHOLE-NUMBER COMPUTATION-MENTAL, ELECTRONIC AND WRITTEN

11. An _____ is a number which is involved in addition. A number being added is considered to be an _____.
    a. A chemical equation
    b. A Mathematical Theory of Communication
    c. A posteriori
    d. Addend

12. _____ is the mathematical operation of scaling one number by another. It is one of the four basic operations in elementary arithmetic.

   _____ is defined for whole numbers in terms of repeated addition; for example, 4 multiplied by 3 can be calculated by adding 3 copies of 4 together:

   $$4 + 4 + 4 = 12.$$

   _____ of rational numbers and real numbers is defined by systematic generalization of this basic idea.

   a. Highest common factor
   b. The number 0 is even.
   c. Least common multiple
   d. Multiplication

13. In mathematics, a _____ can mean either an element of the set {1, 2, 3, ...} (i.e the positive integers) or an element of the set {0, 1, 2, 3, ...} (i.e. the non-negative integers).
    a. Degrees of freedom
    b. Bounded
    c. FISH
    d. Whole number

14. _____ is the calculated approximation of a result which is usable even if input data may be incomplete or uncertain.

   In statistics, see _____ theory, estimator.

   In mathematics, approximation or _____ typically means finding upper or lower bounds of a quantity that cannot readily be computed precisely and is also an educated guess .

   a. Estimation
   b. Estimator
   c. Estimation theory
   d. U-statistic

15. In descriptive statistics, the _____ is the length of the smallest interval which contains all the data. It is calculated by subtracting the smallest observations from the greatest and provides an indication of statistical dispersion.

   It is measured in the same units as the data.

   a. Class
   b. Bandwidth
   c. Kernel
   d. Range

16. In mathematics and computer science, _____ (also base-16, hexa or base, of 16. It uses sixteen distinct symbols, most often the symbols 0-9 to represent values zero to nine, and A, B, C, D, E, F (or a through f) to represent values ten to fifteen.

Chapter 4. WHOLE-NUMBER COMPUTATION-MENTAL, ELECTRONIC AND WRITTEN 33

Its primary use is as a human friendly representation of binary coded values, so it is often used in digital electronics and computer engineering.

a. Factoradic
b. Tetradecimal
c. Hexadecimal
d. Radix

17. In mathematics, an _____ in the sense of ring theory is a subring $\mathcal{O}$ of a ring R that satisfies the conditions

   1. R is a ring which is a finite-dimensional algebra over the rational number field $\mathbb{Q}$
   2. $\mathcal{O}$ spans R over $\mathbb{Q}$, so that $\mathbb{Q}\mathcal{O} = R$, and
   3. $\mathcal{O}$ is a lattice in R.

The third condition can be stated more accurately, in terms of the extension of scalars of R to the real numbers, embedding R in a real vector space. In less formal terms, additively $\mathcal{O}$ should be a free abelian group generated by a basis for R over $\mathbb{Q}$.

The leading example is the case where R is a number field K and $\mathcal{O}$ is its ring of integers. In algebraic number theory there are examples for any K other than the rational field of proper subrings of the ring of integers that are also _____ s.

a. Efficiency
b. Algebraic
c. Annihilator
d. Order

18. In algebra and computer programming, when a number or expression is both preceded and followed by a binary operation, a rule is required for which operation should be applied first; this rule is known as an _____ . From the earliest use of mathematical notation, multiplication took precedence over addition, whichever side of a number it appeared on. Thus 3 + 4 × 5 = 5 × 4 + 3 = 23.

a. Identity element
b. Algebraic K-theory
c. Isomorphism class
d. Order of Operations

19. _____ involves reducing the number of significant digits in a number. The result of _____ is a 'shorter' number having fewer non-zero digits yet similar in magnitude. The result is less precise but easier to use.

a. Sudan function
b. Hyper operator
c. Shabakh
d. Rounding

20. In abstract algebra, a field extension L /K is called _____ if every element of L is _____ over K. Field extensions which are not _____.

For example, the field extension R/Q, that is the field of real numbers as an extension of the field of rational numbers, is transcendental, while the field extensions C/R and Q

a. Algebraic
b. Echo
c. Identity
d. Ideal

Chapter 4. WHOLE-NUMBER COMPUTATION-MENTAL, ELECTRONIC AND WRITTEN

21. In mathematical logic, _____ formalizes logic using the methods of abstract algebra.

_____ treats logics as models of certain algebraic structures, specifically as models of bounded lattices and hence as a branch of order theory.

In _____:

- Variables are tacitly universally quantified over some universe of discourse. There are no existentially quantified variables or open formulas;
- Terms are built up from variables using primitive and defined operations. There are no connectives;
- Formulas, built from terms in the usual way, can be equated if they are logically equivalent. To express a tautology, equate a formula with a truth value;
- The rules of proof are the substitution of equals for equals, and uniform replacement. Modus ponens remains valid, but is seldom employed These structures are either Boolean algebras or proper extensions thereof.

   a. Entailment
   b. Enumerative definition
   c. AND-OR-Invert
   d. Algebraic logic

22. A _____ is a device for performing mathematical calculations, distinguished from a computer by having a limited problem solving ability and an interface optimized for interactive calculation rather than programming. _____s can be hardware or software, and mechanical or electronic, and are often built into devices such as PDAs or mobile phones.

Modern electronic _____s are generally small, digital, and usually inexpensive.

   a. 1-center problem
   b. 120-cell
   c. Calculator
   d. 2-3 heap

23. In vector calculus, _____ is a vector differential operator represented by the nabla symbol: ∇.

_____ is a mathematical tool serving primarily as a convention for mathematical notation; it makes many equations easier to comprehend, write, and remember. Depending on the way _____ is applied, it can describe the gradient (slope), divergence (degree to which something converges or diverges) or curl (rotational motion at points in a fluid.)

   a. Helmholtz decomposition
   b. Vector field reconstruction
   c. Del operator
   d. DEL

24. _____ is the study of the principles of valid demonstration and inference. _____ is a branch of philosophy, a part of the classical trivium of grammar, _____, and rhetoric. of λογικῄς, 'possessed of reason, intellectual, dialectical, argumentative', from λΐŒγος logos, 'word, thought, idea, argument, account, reason, or principle'.
   a. Boolean function
   b. Satisfiability
   c. Counterpart theory
   d. Logic

Chapter 4. WHOLE-NUMBER COMPUTATION-MENTAL, ELECTRONIC AND WRITTEN 35

25. This ordering is called the _____. Another possible ordering on A × B is the lexicographical order.

- direct product of binary relations
- examples of partial orders
- orders on the Cartesian product of totally ordered sets

a. Monte Carlo algorithm
b. Composition of binary relations
c. Product order
d. Digital Morse theory

26. In discrete mathematics and predominantly in set theory, a _____ is a concept used in comparisons of sets to refer to the unique values of one set in relation to another. The terms 'absolute' and 'relative' _____ refer to more specific applications of the concept, with universal _____s referring to elements unique to the universal set and the latter referring to the unique elements of one set in relation to another. In this image, the universal set is represented by the border of the image, and the set A as a disc.

a. Complement
b. Derivative algebra
c. Kernel
d. Huge

27. Exponentiation is a mathematical operation, written a^n, involving two numbers, the base a and the _____ n. When n is a positive integer, exponentiation corresponds to repeated multiplication:

$$a^n = \underbrace{a \times \cdots \times a}_{n},$$

just as multiplication by a positive integer corresponds to repeated addition:

$$a \times n = \underbrace{a + \cdots + a}_{n}.$$

The _____ is usually shown as a superscript to the right of the base. The exponentiation a^n can be read as: a raised to the n-th power, a raised to the power [of] n or possibly a raised to the _____ [of] n, or more briefly: a to the n-th power or a to the power [of] n, or even more briefly: a to the n.

a. Exponential tree
b. Exponential sum
c. Exponent
d. Exponentiating by squaring

28. In mathematics, a _____ is a function whose values do not vary and thus are constant. For example, if we have the function f→ B is a _____ if f

a. Squeeze mapping
b. Point reflection
c. Linear operator
d. Constant function

29. The mathematical concept of a _____ expresses the intuitive idea of deterministic dependence between two quantities, one of which is viewed as primary and the other as secondary. A _____ then is a way to associate a unique output for each input of a specified type, for example, a real number or an element of a given set.

Chapter 4. WHOLE-NUMBER COMPUTATION-MENTAL, ELECTRONIC AND WRITTEN

    a. Going up
    b. Grill
    c. Function
    d. Coherent

30. The x-axis is the horizontal axis of a two- dimensional plot in the _____, that is typically pointed to the right. Also known as a right-handed coordinate system.
    a. 120-cell
    b. 1-center problem
    c. Cartesian coordinate system
    d. 2-3 heap

31. _____, also sometimes known as standard form or as exponential notation, is a way of writing numbers that accommodates values too large or small to be conveniently written in standard decimal notation. _____ has a number of useful properties and is often favored by scientists, mathematicians and engineers, who work with such numbers.

In _____, numbers are written in the form:

$$a \times 10^b$$

    a. Leading zero
    b. 1-center problem
    c. Scientific notation
    d. Radix point

32. In a positional numeral system, the decimal separator is a symbol used to mark the boundary between the integral and the fractional parts of a decimal numeral. When used in context of Arabic numerals, terms implying the symbol used are _____ and decimal comma.

The decimal separator is mathematically a radix point.

    a. Fibonacci coding
    b. Tetradecimal
    c. Hexadecimal
    d. Decimal point

33. In mathematics and physics, there are a _____ number of topics named in honor of Leonhard Euler. As well, many of these topics include their own unique function, equation, formula, identity, number, or other mathematical entity. Unfortunately however, many of these entities have been given simple names like Euler's function, Euler's equation, and Euler's formula, which are further confused by variations of the 'Euler'-prefix Overall though, Euler's work touched upon so many fields that he is often the earliest written reference on a given matter.
    a. List of mathematical knots and links
    b. List of trigonometry topics
    c. List of integrals of logarithmic functions
    d. Large

34. In ecology, predation describes a biological interaction where a _____ (an organism that is hunting) feeds on its prey, the organism that is attacked. _____s may or may not kill their prey prior to feeding on them, but the act of predation always results in the death of the prey. The other main category of consumption is detritivory, the consumption of dead organic material (detritus.)
    a. 1-center problem
    b. Prey
    c. 120-cell
    d. Predator

35. In mathematics, _____ and undefined are used to explain whether or not expressions have meaningful, sensible, and unambiguous values. Not all branches of mathematics come to the same conclusion.

Chapter 4. WHOLE-NUMBER COMPUTATION-MENTAL, ELECTRONIC AND WRITTEN   37

The following expressions are undefined in all contexts, but remarks in the analysis section may apply.

   a. LHS
   c. Plugging in
   b. Toy model
   d. Defined

36. In mathematics, the _____ is an approach to finding a particular solution to certain inhomogeneous ordinary differential equations and recurrence relations. It is closely related to the annihilator method, but instead of using a particular kind of differential operator in order to find the best possible form of the particular solution, a 'guess' is made as to the appropriate form, which is then tested by differentiating the resulting equation. In this sense, the _____ is less formal but more intuitive than the annihilator method.
   a. Linear differential equation
   c. Differential algebraic equations
   b. Phase line
   d. Method of undetermined coefficients

37. In mathematics, a _____ is a picture of a straight line in which the integers are shown as specially-marked points evenly spaced on the line. Although this image only shows the integers from -9 to 9, the line includes all real numbers, continuing 'forever' in each direction. It is often used as an aid in teaching simple addition and subtraction, especially involving negative numbers.
   a. Real number
   c. Number system
   b. Point plotting
   d. Number line

38. _____ is a numeral system in which each position is related to the next by a constant multiplier, a common ratio, called the base or radix of that numeral system.
   a. Cyrillic numerals
   c. Negative base
   b. NegaFibonacci coding
   d. Place value

39. A _____ is an algorithm to multiply two numbers. Depending on the size of the numbers, different algorithms are in use. Efficient _____s have been around since the advent of the decimal system.
   a. Double dabble
   c. Spigot algorithm
   b. Multiplication algorithm
   d. Karatsuba algorithm

40. _____ is a systematic method for multiplying two numbers that does not require the multiplication table, only the ability to multiply and divide by 2, and to add. Also known as Egyptian multiplication and Peasant multiplication, it decomposes one of the multiplicands into a sum of powers of two and creates a table of doublings of the second multiplicand. This method may be called mediation and duplation, where mediation means halving one number and duplation means doubling the other number.
   a. Ancient Egyptian multiplication
   c. A posteriori
   b. A chemical equation
   d. A Mathematical Theory of Communication

41. The _____ are the set of numbers consisting of the natural numbers including 0 and their negatives. They are numbers that can be written without a fractional or decimal component, and fall within the set {... −2, −1, 0, 1, 2, ...}.
   a. A Mathematical Theory of Communication
   c. Integers
   b. A posteriori
   d. A chemical equation

38   Chapter 4. WHOLE-NUMBER COMPUTATION-MENTAL, ELECTRONIC AND WRITTEN

42. In physics, particularly in physics education, a _____, Fermi question approximation, and the importance of clearly identifying one's assumptions. Named for 20th century physicist Enrico Fermi, such problems typically involve making justified guesses about quantities that seem impossible to compute given limited available information.

Fermi was known for his ability to make good approximate calculations with little or no actual data, hence the name.

a. 120-cell
c. 2-3 heap
b. 1-center problem
d. Fermi problem

Chapter 5. NUMBER THEORY

1. In mathematics, a _____ is a mathematical statement which appears resourceful, but has not been formally proven to be true under the rules of mathematical logic. Once a _____ is formally proven true it is elevated to the status of theorem and may be used afterwards without risk in the construction of other formal mathematical proofs. Until that time, mathematicians may use the _____ on a provisional basis, but any resulting work is itself provisional until the underlying _____ is cleared up.
   a. Whitehead conjecture
   b. Moral certainty
   c. Heawood conjecture
   d. Conjecture

2. In mathematics, the _____ of a non-negative integer n, denoted by n!, is the product of all positive integers less than or equal to n. For example,

$$5! = 1 \times 2 \times 3 \times 4 \times 5 = 120$$

and
$$6! = 1 \times 2 \times 3 \times 4 \times 5 \times 6 = 720$$

The notation n! was introduced by Christian Kramp in 1808.

The _____ function is formally defined by

$$n! = \prod_{k=1}^{n} k \qquad \forall n \in \mathbb{N}.$$

The above definition incorporates the instance

$$0! = 1$$

as an instance of the fact that the product of no numbers at all is 1.

   a. Plane partition
   b. Symbolic combinatorics
   c. Partition of a set
   d. Factorial

3. _____ IPA: [pjɛʁ ɛ dɛ™fɛʁ 'ma] (17 August 1601 or 1607/8 - 12 January 1665) was a French lawyer at the Parlement of Toulouse, France, and a mathematician who is given credit for early developments that led to modern calculus. In particular, he is recognized for his discovery of an original method of finding the greatest and the smallest ordinates of curved lines, which is analogous to that of the then unknown differential calculus, as well as his research into the theory of numbers. He also made notable contributions to analytic geometry, probability, and optics.
   a. Nikita Borisov
   b. Philip J. Davis
   c. Felix Hausdorff
   d. Pierre de Fermat

4. _____ is the branch of pure mathematics concerned with the properties of numbers in general, and integers in particular, as well as the wider classes of problems that arise from their study.

Chapter 5. NUMBER THEORY

_____ may be subdivided into several fields, according to the methods used and the type of questions investigated.

The term 'arithmetic' is also used to refer to _____.

   a. Coin problem   b. Number theory
   c. Sociable number   d. Goormaghtigh conjecture

5. In mathematics, a _____ is a statement that can be proved on the basis of explicitly stated or previously agreed assumptions.

   a. Disjunction introduction   b. Logical value
   c. Boolean function   d. Theorem

6. The _____ is a famous unsolved problem in number theory that involves prime numbers. It states:

    There are infinitely many primes p such that p + 2 is also prime.

Such a pair of prime numbers is called a prime twin. The conjecture has been researched by many number theorists.

   a. Character sum   b. Prime number theorem
   c. Legendre sieve   d. Twin prime conjecture

7. In mathematics, in the realm of group theory, a group is said to be _____ if it equals its own commutator subgroup if the group has no nontrivial abelian quotients.

The smallest _____ group is the alternating group A_5. More generally, any non-abelian simple group is _____ since the commutator subgroup is a normal subgroup with abelian quotient.

   a. Perfect   b. Group of Lie type
   c. Quaternion group   d. Free product

8. In mathematics, a _____ is defined as a positive integer which is the sum of its proper positive divisors, that is, the sum of the positive divisors excluding the number itself. Equivalently, a _____ is a number that is half the sum of all of its positive divisors, or = 2n.

The first _____ is 6, because 1, 2, and 3 are its proper positive divisors, and 1 + 2 + 3 = 6.

   a. Blum integer   b. Nonhypotenuse number
   c. Leonardo numbers   d. Perfect number

9. In mathematics, a _____ is a natural number which has exactly two distinct natural number divisors: 1 and itself. An infinitude of _____s exists, as demonstrated by Euclid around 300 BC. The first twenty-five _____s are:

Chapter 5. NUMBER THEORY   41

2, 3, 5, 7, 11, 13, 17, 19, 23, 29, 31, 37, 41, 43, 47, 53, 59, 61, 67, 71, 73, 79, 83, 89, 97.

   a. Pronic number
   c. Perrin number
   b. Highly composite number
   d. Prime number

10. The word _____ has many distinct meanings in different fields of knowledge, depending on their methodologies and the context of discussion. Broadly speaking we can say that a _____ is some kind of belief or claim that (supposedly) explains, asserts, or consolidates some class of claims. Additionally, in contrast with a theorem the statement of the _____ is generally accepted only in some tentative fashion as opposed to regarding it as having been conclusively established.
   a. Per mil
   c. Transport of structure
   b. Defined
   d. Theory

11. In game theory, a player's _____ in a game is a complete plan of action for whatever situation might arise; this fully determines the player's behaviour. A player's _____ will determine the action the player will take at any stage of the game, for every possible history of play up to that stage.

A _____ profile is a set of strategies for each player which fully specifies all actions in a game.

   a. Strategy
   c. Correlated equilibrium
   b. Matching pennies
   d. Sir Philip Sidney game

12. A _____ number is a positive integer which has a positive divisor other than one or itself. By definition, every integer greater than one is either a prime number or a _____ number.zero and one are considered to be neither prime nor _____. For example, the integer 14 is a _____ number because it can be factored as 2 × 7.
   a. Discontinuity
   c. Basis
   b. Key server
   d. Composite

13. A _____ is a positive integer which has a positive divisor other than one or itself. In other words, if 0 < n is an integer and there are integers 1 < a, b < n such that n = a × b then n is composite. By definition, every integer greater than one is either a prime number or a _____.
   a. Ruth-Aaron pair
   c. Megaprime
   b. Composite number
   d. Prime Pages

14. In mathematics, the _____ is a simple, ancient algorithm for finding all prime numbers up to a specified integer. It works efficiently for the smaller primes . It was created by Eratosthenes, an ancient Greek mathematician.
   a. 2-3 heap
   c. Sieve of Eratosthenes
   b. 120-cell
   d. 1-center problem

15. In number theory, the _____ states that every natural number greater than 1 can be written as a unique product of prime numbers. For instance,

$$6936 = 2^3 \times 3 \times 17^2,$$

$$1200 = 2^4 \times 3 \times 5^2.$$

There are no other possible factorizations of 6936 or 1200 into non-negative prime numbers. The above representation collapses repeated prime factors into powers for easier identification.

    a. Fundamental Theorem of Arithmetic
    b. Dedekind sums
    c. Feit–Thompson theorem
    d. Cyclic number

16. In set theory, a _____ is a partially ordered set such that for each t ∈ T, the set {s ∈ T : s < t} is well-ordered by the relation <. For each t ∈ T, the order type of {s ∈ T : s < t} is called the height of t. The height of T itself is the least ordinal greater than the height of each element of T.

    a. Set-theoretic topology
    b. Tree
    c. Definable numbers
    d. Transitive reduction

17. In mathematics, the _____ is a direct product of sets. The _____ is named after René Descartes, whose formulation of analytic geometry gave rise to this concept.

Specifically, the _____ of two sets X and Y, denoted X × Y, is the set of all possible ordered pairs whose first component is a member of X and whose second component is a member of Y:

$$X \times Y = \{(x,y) | x \in X \text{ and } y \in Y\}.$$

For example, the _____ of the 13-element set of standard playing card ranks {Ace, King, Queen, Jack, 10, 9, 8, 7, 6, 5, 4, 3, 2} and the four-element set of card suits {â™ , â™¥, â™¦, â™£} is the 52-element set of all possible playing cards ,, ...,,, ...,}.

    a. Choice function
    b. Disjoint sets
    c. Cartesian product
    d. Set of all sets

18. In mathematics, a _____ of an integer n is an integer which evenly divides n without leaving a remainder.

For example, 7 is a _____ of 42 because 42/7 = 6. We also say 42 is divisible by 7 or 42 is a multiple of 7 or 7 divides 42 or 7 is a factor of 42 and we usually write 7 | 42.

    a. 120-cell
    b. 2-3 heap
    c. Divisor
    d. 1-center problem

Chapter 5. NUMBER THEORY

19. In mathematics, computing, linguistics and related subjects, an _____ is a sequence of finite instructions, often used for calculation and data processing. It is formally a type of effective method in which a list of well-defined instructions for completing a task will, when given an initial state, proceed through a well-defined series of successive states, eventually terminating in an end-state. The transition from one state to the next is not necessarily deterministic; some _____s, known as probabilistic _____s, incorporate randomness.
   - a. In-place algorithm
   - b. Out-of-core
   - c. Approximate counting algorithm
   - d. Algorithm

20. In mathematics, a _____ can mean either an element of the set {1, 2, 3, ...} (i.e the positive integers) or an element of the set {0, 1, 2, 3, ...} (i.e. the non-negative integers).
   - a. Bounded
   - b. Degrees of freedom
   - c. FISH
   - d. Whole number

21. In vascular plants, the _____ is the organ of a plant body that typically lies below the surface of the soil. This is not always the case, however, since a _____ can also be aerial (that is, growing above the ground) or aerating (that is, growing up above the ground or especially above water.) Furthermore, a stem normally occurring below ground is not exceptional either
   - a. 1-center problem
   - b. Root
   - c. 2-3 heap
   - d. 120-cell

22. In mathematics, a _____ of a number x is a number r such that r^2 = x, or, in other words, a number r whose square is x. Every non-negative real number x has a unique non-negative _____, called the principal _____, which is denoted with a radical symbol as $\sqrt{x}$, or, using exponent notation, as $x^{1/2}$. For example, the principal _____ of 9 is 3, denoted $\sqrt{9}$ = 3, because 3^2 = 3 × 3 = 9.
   - a. Square root
   - b. Hyperbolic functions
   - c. Double exponential
   - d. Multiplicative inverse

23. A _____ is a device for performing mathematical calculations, distinguished from a computer by having a limited problem solving ability and an interface optimized for interactive calculation rather than programming. _____s can be hardware or software, and mechanical or electronic, and are often built into devices such as PDAs or mobile phones.

   Modern electronic _____s are generally small, digital, and usually inexpensive.
   - a. 120-cell
   - b. 1-center problem
   - c. 2-3 heap
   - d. Calculator

24. In number theory, the _____s of a positive integer are the prime numbers that divide into that integer exactly, without leaving a remainder. The process of finding these numbers is called integer factorization, or prime factorization.

   For a _____ p of n, the multiplicity of p is the largest exponent a for which p^a divides n.
   - a. Gigantic prime
   - b. Wieferich pair
   - c. Cunningham chain
   - d. Prime factor

Chapter 5. NUMBER THEORY

25. In World War II, _____ was the United States codename for intelligence derived from the cryptanalysis of PURPLE, a Japanese foreign office cipher.

The Japanese and the Germans both used the Enigma machine to encode their cable traffic. The Japanese Enigma-based system was called PURPLE by U.S. cryptographers.

- a. Magic
- b. Basis
- c. Discontinuity
- d. Bandwidth

26. In recreational mathematics, a _____ of order n is an arrangement of n^2 numbers, usually distinct integers, in a square, such that the n numbers in all rows, all columns, and both diagonals sum to the same constant. A normal _____ contains the integers from 1 to n^2. The term '_____' is also sometimes used to refer to any of various types of word square.
- a. 120-cell
- b. Prime reciprocal magic square
- c. Magic square
- d. 1-center problem

27. In mathematics, a _____ is a positive integer that is one less than a power of two:

$$M_n = 2^n - 1.$$

Some definitions of _____s require that the exponent n be prime.

A Mersenne prime is a _____ that is prime. As of October 2008, only 46 Mersenne primes are known; the largest known prime number ($2^{43,112,609} - 1$) is a Mersenne prime, and in modern times, the largest known prime has almost always been a Mersenne prime.

- a. Mersenne number
- b. Red-black tree
- c. Mersenne prime
- d. 1-center problem

28. In number theory, the _____ is an algorithm to determine the greatest common divisor of two elements of any Euclidean domain. Its major significance is that it does not require factoring the two integers, and it is also significant in that it is one of the oldest algorithms known, dating back to the ancient Greeks.

The _____ is one of the oldest algorithms known, since it appeared in Euclid's Elements around 300 BC.

- a. A chemical equation
- b. A Mathematical Theory of Communication
- c. A posteriori
- d. Euclidean algorithm

29. Leonardo of Pisa (c. 1170 - c. 1250), also known as Leonardo Pisano, Leonardo Bonacci, Leonardo _____, or, most commonly, simply _____, was an Italian mathematician, considered by some 'the most talented mathematician of the Middle Ages'.
- a. Fibonacci
- b. Guido Castelnuovo
- c. Harry Hinsley
- d. Ralph C. Merkle

Chapter 5. NUMBER THEORY

30. A _____, from the French patron, is a type of theme of recurring events of or objects, sometimes referred to as elements of a set. These elements repeat in a predictable manner. It can be a template or model which can be used to generate things or parts of a thing, especially if the things that are created have enough in common for the underlying _____ to be inferred, in which case the things are said to exhibit the unique _____.
  a. 120-cell
  b. Pattern
  c. 2-3 heap
  d. 1-center problem

31. In mathematics, the _____ of two sets A and B is the set that contains all elements of A that also belong to B, but no other elements.

For explanation of the symbols used in this article, refer to the table of mathematical symbols.

The _____ of A and B

The _____ of A and B is written 'A ∩ B'. Formally:

> x is an element of A ∩ B if and only if
> - x is an element of A and
> - x is an element of B.
>
> For example:
> - The _____ of the sets {1, 2, 3} and {2, 3, 4} is {2, 3}.
> - The number 9 is not in the _____ of the set of prime numbers {2, 3, 5, 7, 11, â€¦} and the set of odd numbers {1, 3, 5, 7, 9, 11, â€¦}.

If the _____ of two sets A and B is empty, that is they have no elements in common, then they are said to be disjoint, denoted: A ∩ B = Ø. For example the sets {1, 2} and {3, 4} are disjoint, written {1, 2} ∩ {3, 4} = Ø.

  a. Intersection
  b. Advice
  c. Order
  d. Erlang

32. In arithmetic and number theory, the _____ or lowest common multiple or smallest common multiple of two integers a and b is the smallest positive integer that is a multiple of both a and b. Since it is a multiple, it can be divided by a and b without a remainder. If either a or b is 0, so that there is no such positive integer, then lc is defined to be zero.
  a. Plus-minus sign
  b. Least common multiple
  c. Lowest common denominator
  d. Plus and minus signs

33. In mathematics, an _____ or excessive number is a number n for which σσ− 2n is called the abundance of n.
  a. Idoneal number
  b. Integer sequence
  c. Unitary perfect number
  d. Abundant number

34. In mathematics, a _____ or defective number is a number n for which σσ

a. Woodall number
b. Highly totient number
c. Kynea number
d. Deficient number

35. _____ are two different numbers so related that the sum of the proper divisors of one of the numbers is equal to the other, one being considered as a proper divisor but not the number itself. Such a pair is; for the proper divisors of 220 are 1, 2, 4, 5, 10, 11, 20, 22, 44, 55 and 110, of which the sum is 284; and the proper divisors of 284 are 1, 2, 4, 71, and 142, of which the sum is 220. _____ were known to the Pythagoreans, who credited them with many mystical properties.

a. Auxiliary functions
b. Automorphic form
c. Amicable numbers
d. Arithmetic derivative

36. A _____ is a composite number for which, in a given base, the sum of its digits is equal to the sum of the digits in its prime factorization.. For example, 378 = 2 × 3 × 3 × 3 × 7 is a base 10 _____, since 3 + 7 + 8 = 2 + 3 + 3 + 3 + 7. It's important to remember that, by definition, the factors are treated as digits.

a. Smith number
b. Polydivisible number
c. Truncatable prime
d. Self-descriptive number

Chapter 6. FRACTIONS

1. In mathematics, the _____ of a Euclidean space is a special point, usually denoted by the letter O, used as a fixed point of reference for the geometry of the surrounding space. In a Cartesian coordinate system, the _____ is the point where the axes of the system intersect. In Euclidean geometry, the _____ may be chosen freely as any convenient point of reference.
   a. OMAC
   b. Autonomous system
   c. Interval
   d. Origin

2. In the study of metric spaces in mathematics, there are various notions of two metrics on the same underlying space being 'the same', or _____.

In the following, M will denote a non-empty set and d_1 and d_2 will denote two metrics on M.

The two metrics d_1 and d_2 are said to be topologically _____ if they generate the same topology on M.

   a. A Mathematical Theory of Communication
   b. A posteriori
   c. A chemical equation
   d. Equivalent

3. In game theory, a player's _____ in a game is a complete plan of action for whatever situation might arise; this fully determines the player's behaviour. A player's _____ will determine the action the player will take at any stage of the game, for every possible history of play up to that stage.

A _____ profile is a set of strategies for each player which fully specifies all actions in a game.

   a. Correlated equilibrium
   b. Strategy
   c. Sir Philip Sidney game
   d. Matching pennies

4. In mathematics, a set is said to be _____ if the operation on members of the set produces a member of the set. For example, the real numbers are closed under subtraction, but the natural numbers are not: 3 and 7 are both natural numbers, but the result of 3 − 7 is not.

Similarly, a set is said to be closed under a collection of operations if it is closed under each of the operations individually.

   a. Contingency table
   b. Control chart
   c. Continuous linear extension
   d. Closed under some operation

5. In computational complexity theory, the complexity class _____ is the union of the classes in the exponential hierarchy.

$$\begin{aligned} \text{ELEMENTARY} &= \text{EXP} \cup \text{2EXP} \cup \text{3EXP} \cup \cdots \\ &= \text{DTIME}(2^n) \cup \text{DTIME}(2^{2^n}) \cup \text{DTIME}(2^{2^{2^n}}) \cup \cdots \end{aligned}$$

The name was coined by Laszlo Kalmar, in the context of recursive functions and undecidability; most problems in it are far from _____. Some natural recursive problems lie outside _____, and are thus NONELEMENTARY.

a. A posteriori
b. A chemical equation
c. A Mathematical Theory of Communication
d. Elementary

6. _____ consists of mathematics topics frequently taught at the primary and secondary school levels. The most basic are arithmetic and geometry. The next level is probability and statistics, then algebra, then trigonometry and pre-calculus.
   a. Information bottleneck method
   b. Elementary mathematics
   c. Iverson bracket
   d. Exponential error

7. In mathematics, _____ and undefined are used to explain whether or not expressions have meaningful, sensible, and unambiguous values. Not all branches of mathematics come to the same conclusion.

The following expressions are undefined in all contexts, but remarks in the analysis section may apply.

   a. LHS
   b. Toy model
   c. Defined
   d. Plugging in

8. In ecology, predation describes a biological interaction where a _____ (an organism that is hunting) feeds on its prey, the organism that is attacked. _____s may or may not kill their prey prior to feeding on them, but the act of predation always results in the death of the prey. The other main category of consumption is detritivory, the consumption of dead organic material (detritus.)
   a. 120-cell
   b. Prey
   c. Predator
   d. 1-center problem

9. In mathematics, an inequality is a statement about the relative size or order of two objects. For example 14 > 10, or 14 is _____ 10. The notation a > b means that a is _____ b and 'a' would be to the right of 'b' on a number line.
   a. FKG inequality
   b. Minkowski inequality
   c. Greater than
   d. Cauchy-Schwarz inequality

10. In mathematics, a _____ is a picture of a straight line in which the integers are shown as specially-marked points evenly spaced on the line. Although this image only shows the integers from -9 to 9, the line includes all real numbers, continuing 'forever' in each direction. It is often used as an aid in teaching simple addition and subtraction, especially involving negative numbers.
    a. Number system
    b. Point plotting
    c. Number line
    d. Real number

11. In mathematics, an _____ is a statement about the relative size or order of two objects, or about whether they are the same or not

   - The notation a < b means that a is less than b.
   - The notation a > b means that a is greater than b.
   - The notation a ≠ b means that a is not equal to b, but does not say that one is bigger than the other or even that they can be compared in size.

In all these cases, a is not equal to b, hence, '_____'.

Chapter 6. FRACTIONS

These relations are known as strict _____

- The notation a ≤ b means that a is less than or equal to b;
- The notation a ≥ b means that a is greater than or equal to b;

An additional use of the notation is to show that one quantity is much greater than another, normally by several orders of magnitude.

- The notation a << b means that a is much less than b.
- The notation a >> b means that a is much greater than b.

If the sense of the _____ is the same for all values of the variables for which its members are defined, then the _____ is called an 'absolute' or 'unconditional' _____. If the sense of an _____ holds only for certain values of the variables involved, but is reversed or destroyed for other values of the variables, it is called a conditional _____.

An _____ may appear unsolvable because it only states whether a number is larger or smaller than another number; but it is possible to apply the same operations for equalities to inequalities. For example, to find x for the _____ 10x > 23 one would divide 23 by 10.

a. A chemical equation
b. Inequality
c. A Mathematical Theory of Communication
d. A posteriori

12. The _____ of a material is defined as its mass per unit volume:

$$\rho = \frac{m}{V}$$

Different materials usually have different densities, so _____ is an important concept regarding buoyancy, metal purity and packaging.

In some cases _____ is expressed as the dimensionless quantities specific gravity or relative _____, in which case it is expressed in multiples of the _____ of some other standard material, usually water or air.

In a well-known story, Archimedes was given the task of determining whether King Hiero's goldsmith was embezzling gold during the manufacture of a wreath dedicated to the gods and replacing it with another, cheaper alloy.

a. 120-cell
b. 1-center problem
c. 2-3 heap
d. Density

13. _____ is the likelihood or chance that something is the case or will happen. Theoretical _____ is used extensively in areas such as statistics, mathematics, science and philosophy to draw conclusions about the likelihood of potential events and the underlying mechanics of complex systems.

The word _____ does not have a consistent direct definition.

a. Standardized moment
b. Probability
c. Statistical significance
d. Discrete random variable

14. An _____ is a number which is involved in addition. A number being added is considered to be an _____.
a. A posteriori
b. A Mathematical Theory of Communication
c. A chemical equation
d. Addend

15. In mathematics, the _____ or least common denominator is the least common multiple of the denominators of a set of vulgar fractions. It is the smallest positive integer that is a multiple of the denominators. For instance, the _____ of

$$\left\{\frac{5}{12}, \frac{11}{18}\right\}$$

is 36 because the least common multiple of 12 and 18 is 36.

a. The number 0 is even.
b. Subtrahend
c. Highest common factor
d. Lowest common denominator

16. A _____ is a device for performing mathematical calculations, distinguished from a computer by having a limited problem solving ability and an interface optimized for interactive calculation rather than programming. _____s can be hardware or software, and mechanical or electronic, and are often built into devices such as PDAs or mobile phones.

Modern electronic _____s are generally small, digital, and usually inexpensive.

a. 1-center problem
b. 2-3 heap
c. Calculator
d. 120-cell

17. In vector calculus, _____ is a vector differential operator represented by the nabla symbol: ∇.

_____ is a mathematical tool serving primarily as a convention for mathematical notation; it makes many equations easier to comprehend, write, and remember. Depending on the way _____ is applied, it can describe the gradient (slope), divergence (degree to which something converges or diverges) or curl (rotational motion at points in a fluid.)

a. Helmholtz decomposition
b. Del operator
c. Vector field reconstruction
d. DEL

Chapter 6. FRACTIONS

18. In mathematics the _____ of a set which is equipped with the operation of addition is an element which, when added to any element x in the set, yields x. One of the most familiar additive identities is the number 0 from elementary mathematics, but additive identities occur in other mathematical structures where addition is defined, such as in groups and rings.

- The _____ familiar from elementary mathematics is zero, denoted 0. For example,

5 + 0 = 5 = 0 + 5.

- In the natural numbers N and all of its supersets, the _____ is 0. Thus for any one of these numbers n,

n + 0 = n = 0 + n.

Let N be a set which is closed under the operation of addition, denoted +. An _____ for N is any element e such that for any element n in N,

e + n = n = n + e.

a. Unit ring
c. Unique factorization domain
b. Algebraically independent
d. Additive identity

19. In mathematics, _____ is a property that a binary operation can have. It means that, within an expression containing two or more of the same associative operators in a row, the order that the operations are performed does not matter as long as the sequence of the operands is not changed. That is, rearranging the parentheses in such an expression will not change its value.
a. Unital
c. Associativity
b. Idempotence
d. Algebraically closed

20. The _____ is a rule which states that when you add or multiply numbers, changing the order doesn't change the result.
a. Conditional event algebra
c. Semigroupoid
b. Coimage
d. Commutative law

21. In mathematics, the term _____ has several different important meanings:

- An _____ is an equality that remains true regardless of the values of any variables that appear within it, to distinguish it from an equality which is true under more particular conditions. For this, the 'triple bar' symbol ≡ is sometimes used.
- In algebra, an _____ or _____ element of a set S with a binary operation Â· is an element e that, when combined with any element x of S, produces that same x. That is, eÂ·x = xÂ·e = x for all x in S.
    - The _____ function from a set S to itself, often denoted id or id_S, s the function such that i = x for all x in S. This function serves as the _____ element in the set of all functions from S to itself with respect to function composition.
    - In linear algebra, the _____ matrix of size n is the n-by-n square matrix with ones on the main diagonal and zeros elsewhere. This matrix serves as the _____ with respect to matrix multiplication.

A common example of the first meaning is the trigonometric _____

$$\sin^2 \theta + \cos^2 \theta = 1$$

which is true for all real values of θ, as opposed to

$$\cos \theta = 1,$$

which is true only for some values of θ, not all. For example, the latter equation is true when $\theta = 0$, false when $\theta = 2$

The concepts of 'additive _____' and 'multiplicative _____' are central to the Peano axioms. The number 0 is the 'additive _____' for integers, real numbers, and complex numbers. For the real numbers, for all $a \in \mathbb{R}$,

$$0 + a = a,$$

$$a + 0 = a, \text{ and}$$

$$0 + 0 = 0.$$

Similarly, The number 1 is the 'multiplicative _____' for integers, real numbers, and complex numbers.

a. Intersection
b. Action
c. Identity
d. ARIA

22. In discrete mathematics and predominantly in set theory, a _____ is a concept used in comparisons of sets to refer to the unique values of one set in relation to another. The terms 'absolute' and 'relative' _____ refer to more specific applications of the concept, with universal _____s referring to elements unique to the universal set and the latter referring to the unique elements of one set in relation to another. In this image, the universal set is represented by the border of the image, and the set A as a disc.

a. Huge
b. Derivative algebra
c. Kernel
d. Complement

23. _____ is the calculated approximation of a result which is usable even if input data may be incomplete or uncertain.

In statistics, see _____ theory, estimator.

In mathematics, approximation or _____ typically means finding upper or lower bounds of a quantity that cannot readily be computed precisely and is also an educated guess .

Chapter 6. FRACTIONS

a. Estimator
b. U-statistic
c. Estimation theory
d. Estimation

24. _____ involves reducing the number of significant digits in a number. The result of _____ is a 'shorter' number having fewer non-zero digits yet similar in magnitude. The result is less precise but easier to use.
    a. Shabakh
    b. Sudan function
    c. Hyper operator
    d. Rounding

25. In mathematics, a _____ is a series with a constant ratio between successive terms. For example, the series

$$\frac{1}{2} + \frac{1}{4} + \frac{1}{8} + \frac{1}{16} + \cdots$$

is geometric, because each term is equal to half of the previous term. The sum of this series is 1, as illustrated in the following picture:

_____ are one of the simplest examples of infinite series with finite sums.

   a. Riemann series theorem
   b. Summation by parts
   c. Telescoping series
   d. Geometric series

26. In acoustics and telecommunication, the _____ of a wave is a component frequency of the signal that is an integer multiple of the fundamental frequency. For example, if the frequency is f, the _____s have frequency 2f, 3f, 4f, etc, as well as f itself. The _____s have the property that they are all periodic at the signal frequency.
    a. Digital room correction
    b. Robinson-Dadson curves
    c. Harmonic
    d. Subharmonic

27. In mathematics, a _____ is often represented as the sum of a sequence of terms. That is, a _____ is represented as a list of numbers with addition operations between them, for example this arithmetic sequence:

   1 + 2 + 3 + 4 + 5 + ... + 99 + 100

In most cases of interest the terms of the sequence are produced according to a certain rule, such as by a formula, by an algorithm, by a sequence of measurements, or even by a random number generator.

   a. Concavity
   b. Blind
   c. Contact
   d. Series

28. A _____ is one of the basic shapes of geometry: a polygon with three corners or vertices and three sides or edges which are line segments. A _____ with vertices A, B, and C is denoted ABC.

In Euclidean geometry any three non-collinear points determine a unique _____ and a unique plane.

a. Kepler triangle
b. Fuhrmann circle
c. 1-center problem
d. Triangle

29. _____ is the mathematical operation of scaling one number by another. It is one of the four basic operations in elementary arithmetic.

_____ is defined for whole numbers in terms of repeated addition; for example, 4 multiplied by 3 can be calculated by adding 3 copies of 4 together:

$$4 + 4 + 4 = 12.$$

_____ of rational numbers and real numbers is defined by systematic generalization of this basic idea.

a. Highest common factor
b. The number 0 is even.
c. Multiplication
d. Least common multiple

30. The _____ are the set of numbers consisting of the natural numbers including 0 and their negatives. They are numbers that can be written without a fractional or decimal component, and fall within the set {... −2, −1, 0, 1, 2, ...}.

a. A posteriori
b. A Mathematical Theory of Communication
c. Integers
d. A chemical equation

31. In computational complexity theory, an algorithm is said to take _____ if the asymptotic upper bound for the time it requires is proportional to the size of the input, which is usually denoted n.

Informally spoken, the running time increases linearly with the size of the input. For example, a procedure that adds up all elements of a list requires time proportional to the length of the list.

a. Constructible function
b. Time-constructible function
c. Linear time
d. Truth table reduction

32. In mathematics, a _____ can mean either an element of the set {1, 2, 3, ...} (i.e the positive integers) or an element of the set {0, 1, 2, 3, ...} (i.e. the non-negative integers).

a. FISH
b. Degrees of freedom
c. Bounded
d. Whole number

33. In mathematics, the _____ is a direct product of sets. The _____ is named after René Descartes, whose formulation of analytic geometry gave rise to this concept.

Specifically, the _____ of two sets X and Y, denoted X × Y, is the set of all possible ordered pairs whose first component is a member of X and whose second component is a member of Y:

$$X \times Y = \{(x,y) | x \in X \text{ and } y \in Y\}.$$

Chapter 6. FRACTIONS

For example, the _____ of the 13-element set of standard playing card ranks {Ace, King, Queen, Jack, 10, 9, 8, 7, 6, 5, 4, 3, 2} and the four-element set of card suits {♠, ♥, ♦, ♣} is the 52-element set of all possible playing cards ,, ...,,, ...,,}.

- a. Choice function
- b. Cartesian product
- c. Set of all sets
- d. Disjoint sets

34. In mathematics, the _____ of a number n is the number that, when added to n, yields zero. The _____ of n is denoted −n. For example, 7 is −7, because 7 + (−7) = 0, and the _____ of −0.3 is 0.3, because −0.3 + 0.3 = 0.
- a. Arity
- b. Algebraic structure
- c. Associativity
- d. Additive inverse

35. A _____ is an algorithm to multiply two numbers. Depending on the size of the numbers, different algorithms are in use. Efficient _____s have been around since the advent of the decimal system.
- a. Double dabble
- b. Karatsuba algorithm
- c. Spigot algorithm
- d. Multiplication algorithm

36. In mathematics, a _____ for a number x, denoted by $\frac{1}{x}$ or x^{-1}, is a number which when multiplied by x yields the multiplicative identity, 1. The _____ of x is also called the reciprocal of x. The _____ of a fraction p/q is q/p.
- a. Golden function
- b. Hyperbolic function
- c. Double exponential
- d. Multiplicative inverse

37. In mathematics, computing, linguistics and related subjects, an _____ is a sequence of finite instructions, often used for calculation and data processing. It is formally a type of effective method in which a list of well-defined instructions for completing a task will, when given an initial state, proceed through a well-defined series of successive states, eventually terminating in an end-state. The transition from one state to the next is not necessarily deterministic; some _____s, known as probabilistic _____s, incorporate randomness.
- a. Algorithm
- b. Approximate counting algorithm
- c. In-place algorithm
- d. Out-of-core

38. In mathematics, the multiplicative inverse of a number x, denoted 1/x or x^{-1}, is the number which, when multiplied by x, yields 1. The multiplicative inverse of x is also called the _____ of x.
- a. 120-cell
- b. Reciprocal
- c. 1-center problem
- d. 2-3 heap

39. In mathematics, and in particular in abstract algebra, distributivity is a property of binary operations that generalises the _____ law from elementary algebra.
- a. Distributive
- b. Closure with a twist
- c. General linear group
- d. Permutation

Chapter 7. DECIMALS, RATIO, PROPORTION, AND PERCENT

1. In mathematics and the arts, two quantities are in the _____ if the ratio between the sum of those quantities and the larger one is the same as the ratio between the larger one and the smaller. The _____ is an irrational mathematical constant, approximately 1.6180339887.

At least since the Renaissance, many artists and architects have proportioned their works to approximate the _____ -- especially in the form of the golden rectangle, in which the ratio of the longer side to the shorter is the _____ --believing this proportion to be aesthetically pleasing.

   a. 2-3 heap
   b. 120-cell
   c. 1-center problem
   d. Golden ratio

2. _____ is a special mathematical relationship between two quantities. Two quantities are called proportional if they vary in such a way that one of the quantities is a constant multiple of the other, or equivalently if they have a constant ratio.
   a. Compression
   b. Depth
   c. Proportionality
   d. Discontinuity

3. In geometry, a _____ is defined as a quadrilateral where all four of its angles are right angles.
   a. Cantor-Dedekind axiom
   b. Polytope
   c. Rectangle
   d. Point group in two dimensions

4. A _____ is one of the basic shapes of geometry: a polygon with three corners or vertices and three sides or edges which are line segments. A _____ with vertices A, B, and C is denoted ABC.

In Euclidean geometry any three non-collinear points determine a unique _____ and a unique plane.

   a. Fuhrmann circle
   b. 1-center problem
   c. Kepler triangle
   d. Triangle

5. In game theory, a player's _____ in a game is a complete plan of action for whatever situation might arise; this fully determines the player's behaviour. A player's _____ will determine the action the player will take at any stage of the game, for every possible history of play up to that stage.

A _____ profile is a set of strategies for each player which fully specifies all actions in a game.

   a. Matching pennies
   b. Correlated equilibrium
   c. Sir Philip Sidney game
   d. Strategy

6. In ecology, predation describes a biological interaction where a _____ (an organism that is hunting) feeds on its prey, the organism that is attacked. _____ s may or may not kill their prey prior to feeding on them, but the act of predation always results in the death of the prey. The other main category of consumption is detritivory, the consumption of dead organic material (detritus.)
   a. Prey
   b. Predator
   c. 120-cell
   d. 1-center problem

7. In a positional numeral system, the decimal separator is a symbol used to mark the boundary between the integral and the fractional parts of a decimal numeral. When used in context of Arabic numerals, terms implying the symbol used are _____ and decimal comma.

Chapter 7. DECIMALS, RATIO, PROPORTION, AND PERCENT

The decimal separator is mathematically a radix point.

a. Fibonacci coding
b. Hexadecimal
c. Decimal point
d. Tetradecimal

8. In mathematics, _____ and undefined are used to explain whether or not expressions have meaningful, sensible, and unambiguous values. Not all branches of mathematics come to the same conclusion.

The following expressions are undefined in all contexts, but remarks in the analysis section may apply.

a. Toy model
b. Plugging in
c. Defined
d. LHS

9. _____ is simply the manner of writing out an expression in full. When a quantity is written as a sum of terms, or as a continued product, _____ notation is used to illustrate the expression in its entirety.

a. Algebraic function
b. Algebraic element
c. Algebra
d. Expanded form

10. In mathematics, a _____ is a picture of a straight line in which the integers are shown as specially-marked points evenly spaced on the line. Although this image only shows the integers from -9 to 9, the line includes all real numbers, continuing 'forever' in each direction. It is often used as an aid in teaching simple addition and subtraction, especially involving negative numbers.

a. Point plotting
b. Number system
c. Real number
d. Number line

11. A _____ of a non-negative real number r is an expression of the form

$$r = \sum_{i=0}^{\infty} \frac{a_i}{10^i}$$

where a_0 is a nonnegative integer, and $a_1, a_2, \ldots$ are integers satisfying $0 \leq a_i \leq 9$; this is often written more briefly as

$$r = a_0.a_1 a_2 a_3 \ldots.$$

That is to say, a_0 is the integer part of r, not necessarily between 0 and 9, and $a_1, a_2, a_3, \ldots$ are the digits forming the fractional part of r.

Any real number can be approximated to any desired degree of accuracy by rational numbers with finite _____s.

Chapter 7. DECIMALS, RATIO, PROPORTION, AND PERCENT

Assume $x \geq 0$. Then for every integer $n \geq 1$ there is a finite decimal $r_n = a_0.a_1 a_2 \cdots a_n$ such that

$$r_n \leq x < r_n + \frac{1}{10^n}.$$

Proof:

Let $r_n = \frac{p}{10^n}$, where $p = \lfloor 10^n x \rfloor$.

a. 2-3 heap
b. 1-center problem
c. 120-cell
d. Decimal representation

12. _____ is the calculated approximation of a result which is usable even if input data may be incomplete or uncertain.

In statistics, see _____ theory, estimator.

In mathematics, approximation or _____ typically means finding upper or lower bounds of a quantity that cannot readily be computed precisely and is also an educated guess .

a. Estimator
b. U-statistic
c. Estimation
d. Estimation theory

13. In mathematics, a set is said to be _____ if the operation on members of the set produces a member of the set. For example, the real numbers are closed under subtraction, but the natural numbers are not: 3 and 7 are both natural numbers, but the result of 3 − 7 is not.

Similarly, a set is said to be closed under a collection of operations if it is closed under each of the operations individually.

a. Continuous linear extension
b. Closed under some operation
c. Control chart
d. Contingency table

14. Exponentiation is a mathematical operation, written a^n, involving two numbers, the base a and the _____ n. When n is a positive integer, exponentiation corresponds to repeated multiplication:

$$a^n = \underbrace{a \times \cdots \times a}_{n},$$

just as multiplication by a positive integer corresponds to repeated addition:

$$a \times n = \underbrace{a + \cdots + a}_{n}.$$

The _____ is usually shown as a superscript to the right of the base. The exponentiation a^n can be read as: a raised to the n-th power, a raised to the power [of] n or possibly a raised to the _____ [of] n, or more briefly: a to the n-th power or a to the power [of] n, or even more briefly: a to the n.

- a. Exponentiating by squaring
- b. Exponential sum
- c. Exponential tree
- d. Exponent

15. _____ involves reducing the number of significant digits in a number. The result of _____ is a 'shorter' number having fewer non-zero digits yet similar in magnitude. The result is less precise but easier to use.
- a. Hyper operator
- b. Shabakh
- c. Rounding
- d. Sudan function

16. In mathematics, computing, linguistics and related subjects, an _____ is a sequence of finite instructions, often used for calculation and data processing. It is formally a type of effective method in which a list of well-defined instructions for completing a task will, when given an initial state, proceed through a well-defined series of successive states, eventually terminating in an end-state. The transition from one state to the next is not necessarily deterministic; some _____s, known as probabilistic _____s, incorporate randomness.
- a. Out-of-core
- b. In-place algorithm
- c. Approximate counting algorithm
- d. Algorithm

17. A _____ is a device for performing mathematical calculations, distinguished from a computer by having a limited problem solving ability and an interface optimized for interactive calculation rather than programming. _____s can be hardware or software, and mechanical or electronic, and are often built into devices such as PDAs or mobile phones.

Modern electronic _____s are generally small, digital, and usually inexpensive.

- a. 1-center problem
- b. Calculator
- c. 2-3 heap
- d. 120-cell

18. An _____ is a number which is involved in addition. A number being added is considered to be an _____.
- a. A posteriori
- b. Addend
- c. A Mathematical Theory of Communication
- d. A chemical equation

19. In discrete mathematics and predominantly in set theory, a _____ is a concept used in comparisons of sets to refer to the unique values of one set in relation to another. The terms 'absolute' and 'relative' _____ refer to more specific applications of the concept, with universal _____s referring to elements unique to the universal set and the latter referring to the unique elements of one set in relation to another. In this image, the universal set is represented by the border of the image, and the set A as a disc.

Chapter 7. DECIMALS, RATIO, PROPORTION, AND PERCENT

a. Huge
b. Derivative algebra
c. Kernel
d. Complement

20. _____ is the mathematical operation of scaling one number by another. It is one of the four basic operations in elementary arithmetic.

_____ is defined for whole numbers in terms of repeated addition; for example, 4 multiplied by 3 can be calculated by adding 3 copies of 4 together:

$$4 + 4 + 4 = 12.$$

_____ of rational numbers and real numbers is defined by systematic generalization of this basic idea.

a. Highest common factor
b. Least common multiple
c. The number 0 is even.
d. Multiplication

21. In mathematics, a _____ can mean either an element of the set {1, 2, 3, ...} (i.e the positive integers) or an element of the set {0, 1, 2, 3, ...} (i.e. the non-negative integers).
a. Bounded
b. FISH
c. Degrees of freedom
d. Whole number

22. The _____ are the set of numbers consisting of the natural numbers including 0 and their negatives. They are numbers that can be written without a fractional or decimal component, and fall within the set {... −2, −1, 0, 1, 2, ...}.
a. A chemical equation
b. A posteriori
c. A Mathematical Theory of Communication
d. Integers

23. In mathematics, a _____ is a number that can be expressed as an integral of an algebraic function over an algebraic domain. Kontsevich and Zagier define a _____ as a complex number whose real and imaginary parts are values of absolutely convergent integrals of rational functions with rational coefficients, over domains in given by polynomial inequalities with rational coefficients.
a. Disk
b. Boussinesq approximation
c. Closeness
d. Period

24. A _____, from the French patron, is a type of theme of recurring events of or objects, sometimes referred to as elements of a set. These elements repeat in a predictable manner. It can be a template or model which can be used to generate things or parts of a thing, especially if the things that are created have enough in common for the underlying _____ to be inferred, in which case the things are said to exhibit the unique _____.
a. 2-3 heap
b. 120-cell
c. 1-center problem
d. Pattern

25. A _____ is a dynamic set of visual, auditory, or tactile symbols of communication and the elements used to manipulate them. _____ can also refer to the use of such systems as a general phenomenon. Strictly speaking, _____ is considered to be an exclusively human mode of communication.
a. 2-3 heap
b. 120-cell
c. Language
d. 1-center problem

Chapter 7. DECIMALS, RATIO, PROPORTION, AND PERCENT

26. _____, also sometimes known as standard form or as exponential notation, is a way of writing numbers that accommodates values too large or small to be conveniently written in standard decimal notation. _____ has a number of useful properties and is often favored by scientists, mathematicians and engineers, who work with such numbers.

In _____, numbers are written in the form:

$$a \times 10^b$$

a. Radix point
b. Leading zero
c. 1-center problem
d. Scientific notation

27. In the study of metric spaces in mathematics, there are various notions of two metrics on the same underlying space being 'the same', or _____.

In the following, M will denote a non-empty set and d_1 and d_2 will denote two metrics on M.

The two metrics d_1 and d_2 are said to be topologically _____ if they generate the same topology on M.

a. A Mathematical Theory of Communication
b. A chemical equation
c. A posteriori
d. Equivalent

28. In statistics, _____ has two related meanings:

- the arithmetic _____.
- the expected value of a random variable, which is also called the population _____.

It is sometimes stated that the '_____' _____s average. This is incorrect if '_____' is taken in the specific sense of 'arithmetic _____' as there are different types of averages: the _____, median, and mode. For instance, average house prices almost always use the median value for the average.

For a real-valued random variable X, the _____ is the expectation of X.

a. Proportional hazards model
b. Probability
c. Statistical population
d. Mean

29. In mathematics, an _____, or central tendency of a data set refers to a measure of the 'middle' or 'expected' value of the data set. There are many different descriptive statistics that can be chosen as a measurement of the central tendency of the data items.

An _____ is a single value that is meant to typify a list of values.

a. Average
b. A chemical equation
c. A posteriori
d. A Mathematical Theory of Communication

Chapter 7. DECIMALS, RATIO, PROPORTION, AND PERCENT

30. In mathematics and computer science, _____ (also base-16, hexa or base, of 16. It uses sixteen distinct symbols, most often the symbols 0-9 to represent values zero to nine, and A, B, C, D, E, F (or a through f) to represent values ten to fifteen.

Its primary use is as a human friendly representation of binary coded values, so it is often used in digital electronics and computer engineering.

    a. Hexadecimal   b. Tetradecimal
    c. Factoradic   d. Radix

31. In mathematics, the _____ of a Euclidean space is a special point, usually denoted by the letter O, used as a fixed point of reference for the geometry of the surrounding space. In a Cartesian coordinate system, the _____ is the point where the axes of the system intersect. In Euclidean geometry, the _____ may be chosen freely as any convenient point of reference.

    a. Interval   b. OMAC
    c. Autonomous system   d. Origin

32. _____ is a fee, paid on borrowed capital. Assets lent include money, shares, consumer goods through hire purchase, major assets such as aircraft, and even entire factories in finance lease arrangements. The _____ is calculated upon the value of the assets in the same manner as upon money.

    a. A Mathematical Theory of Communication   b. Interest sensitivity gap
    c. Interest expense   d. Interest

33. In mathematics, an _____ is a statement about the relative size or order of two objects, or about whether they are the same or not

- The notation a < b means that a is less than b.
- The notation a > b means that a is greater than b.
- The notation a ≠ b means that a is not equal to b, but does not say that one is bigger than the other or even that they can be compared in size.

In all these cases, a is not equal to b, hence, '_____'.

These relations are known as strict _____

- The notation a ≤ b means that a is less than or equal to b;
- The notation a ≥ b means that a is greater than or equal to b;

An additional use of the notation is to show that one quantity is much greater than another, normally by several orders of magnitude.

- The notation a << b means that a is much less than b.
- The notation a >> b means that a is much greater than b.

Chapter 7. DECIMALS, RATIO, PROPORTION, AND PERCENT

If the sense of the _____ is the same for all values of the variables for which its members are defined, then the _____ is called an 'absolute' or 'unconditional' _____. If the sense of an _____ holds only for certain values of the variables involved, but is reversed or destroyed for other values of the variables, it is called a conditional _____.

An _____ may appear unsolvable because it only states whether a number is larger or smaller than another number; but it is possible to apply the same operations for equalities to inequalities. For example, to find x for the _____ 10x > 23 one would divide 23 by 10.

a. Inequality
b. A Mathematical Theory of Communication
c. A posteriori
d. A chemical equation

34. In mathematics, the _____ of a number n is the number that, when added to n, yields zero. The _____ of n is denoted −n. For example, 7 is −7, because 7 + (−7) = 0, and the _____ of −0.3 is 0.3, because −0.3 + 0.3 = 0.
a. Additive inverse
b. Arity
c. Associativity
d. Algebraic structure

Chapter 8. INTEGERS

1. In mathematics, an _____ or member of a set is any one of the distinct objects that make up that set.

Writing A = {1,2,3,4}, means that the _____s of the set A are the numbers 1, 2, 3 and 4. Groups of _____s of A, for example {1,2}, are subsets of A.

   a. Order
   b. Ideal
   c. Universal code
   d. Element

2. The _____ are the set of numbers consisting of the natural numbers including 0 and their negatives. They are numbers that can be written without a fractional or decimal component, and fall within the set {... −2, −1, 0, 1, 2, ...}.
   a. Integers
   b. A chemical equation
   c. A Mathematical Theory of Communication
   d. A posteriori

3. In game theory, a player's _____ in a game is a complete plan of action for whatever situation might arise; this fully determines the player's behaviour. A player's _____ will determine the action the player will take at any stage of the game, for every possible history of play up to that stage.

A _____ profile is a set of strategies for each player which fully specifies all actions in a game.

   a. Matching pennies
   b. Sir Philip Sidney game
   c. Correlated equilibrium
   d. Strategy

4. An _____ is a number which is involved in addition. A number being added is considered to be an _____.
   a. Addend
   b. A Mathematical Theory of Communication
   c. A posteriori
   d. A chemical equation

5. In ecology, predation describes a biological interaction where a _____ (an organism that is hunting) feeds on its prey, the organism that is attacked. _____s may or may not kill their prey prior to feeding on them, but the act of predation always results in the death of the prey. The other main category of consumption is detritivory, the consumption of dead organic material (detritus.)
   a. Prey
   b. 1-center problem
   c. 120-cell
   d. Predator

6. In mathematics, a _____ is a picture of a straight line in which the integers are shown as specially-marked points evenly spaced on the line. Although this image only shows the integers from -9 to 9, the line includes all real numbers, continuing 'forever' in each direction. It is often used as an aid in teaching simple addition and subtraction, especially involving negative numbers.
   a. Number line
   b. Number system
   c. Point plotting
   d. Real number

7. In mathematics, the _____ of a number n is the number that, when added to n, yields zero. The _____ of n is denoted −n. For example, 7 is −7, because 7 + (−7) = 0, and the _____ of −0.3 is 0.3, because −0.3 + 0.3 = 0.
   a. Algebraic structure
   b. Associativity
   c. Arity
   d. Additive inverse

8. In mathematics, _____ and undefined are used to explain whether or not expressions have meaningful, sensible, and unambiguous values. Not all branches of mathematics come to the same conclusion.

The following expressions are undefined in all contexts, but remarks in the analysis section may apply.

a. LHS
b. Toy model
c. Plugging in
d. Defined

9. The framework of quantum mechanics requires a careful definition of _____, and a thorough discussion of its practical and philosophical implications.

_____ is viewed in different ways in the many interpretations of quantum mechanics; however, despite the considerable philosophical differences, they almost universally agree on the practical question of what results from a routine quantum-physics laboratory _____. To describe this, a simple framework to use is the Copenhagen interpretation, and it will be implicitly used in this section; the utility of this approach has been verified countless times, and all other interpretations are necessarily constructed so as to give the same quantitative predictions as this in almost every case.

a. 1-center problem
b. Fundamental units
c. Dynamic range
d. Measurement

10. In mathematics the _____ of a set which is equipped with the operation of addition is an element which, when added to any element x in the set, yields x. One of the most familiar additive identities is the number 0 from elementary mathematics, but additive identities occur in other mathematical structures where addition is defined, such as in groups and rings.

- The _____ familiar from elementary mathematics is zero, denoted 0. For example,

    $5 + 0 = 5 = 0 + 5$.

- In the natural numbers N and all of its supersets, the _____ is 0. Thus for any one of these numbers n,

    $n + 0 = n = 0 + n$.

Let N be a set which is closed under the operation of addition, denoted +. An _____ for N is any element e such that for any element n in N,

$e + n = n = n + e$.

a. Algebraically independent
b. Unique factorization domain
c. Additive identity
d. Unit ring

11. In mathematics, _____ is a property that a binary operation can have. It means that, within an expression containing two or more of the same associative operators in a row, the order that the operations are performed does not matter as long as the sequence of the operands is not changed. That is, rearranging the parentheses in such an expression will not change its value.

a. Idempotence
b. Unital
c. Algebraically closed
d. Associativity

12. In mathematics, a set is said to be _____ if the operation on members of the set produces a member of the set. For example, the real numbers are closed under subtraction, but the natural numbers are not: 3 and 7 are both natural numbers, but the result of 3 − 7 is not.

Similarly, a set is said to be closed under a collection of operations if it is closed under each of the operations individually.

a. Control chart
b. Continuous linear extension
c. Closed under some operation
d. Contingency table

13. The _____ is a rule which states that when you add or multiply numbers, changing the order doesn't change the result.

a. Conditional event algebra
b. Coimage
c. Commutative law
d. Semigroupoid

14. In mathematics, the term _____ has several different important meanings:

- An _____ is an equality that remains true regardless of the values of any variables that appear within it, to distinguish it from an equality which is true under more particular conditions. For this, the 'triple bar' symbol ≡ is sometimes used.
- In algebra, an _____ or _____ element of a set S with a binary operation Â· is an element e that, when combined with any element x of S, produces that same x. That is, eÂ·x = xÂ·e = x for all x in S.
    - The _____ function from a set S to itself, often denoted id or id$_S$, s the function such that i = x for all x in S. This function serves as the _____ element in the set of all functions from S to itself with respect to function composition.
    - In linear algebra, the _____ matrix of size n is the n-by-n square matrix with ones on the main diagonal and zeros elsewhere. This matrix serves as the _____ with respect to matrix multiplication.

A common example of the first meaning is the trigonometric _____

$$\sin^2 \theta + \cos^2 \theta = 1$$

which is true for all real values of θ, as opposed to

$$\cos \theta = 1,$$

which is true only for some values of θ, not all. For example, the latter equation is true when $\theta = 0$, false when $\theta = 2$

Chapter 8. INTEGERS

The concepts of 'additive _____' and 'multiplicative _____' are central to the Peano axioms. The number 0 is the 'additive _____' for integers, real numbers, and complex numbers. For the real numbers, for all $a \in \mathbb{R}$,

$$0 + a = a,$$

$$a + 0 = a,\text{ and}$$

$$0 + 0 = 0.$$

Similarly, The number 1 is the 'multiplicative _____' for integers, real numbers, and complex numbers.

a. ARIA
b. Intersection
c. Identity
d. Action

15. In mathematics, the notion of cancellative is a generalization of the notion of invertible.

An element a in a magma has the left _____ if for all b and c in M, a * b = a * c always implies b = c.

An element a in a magma has the right _____ if for all b and c in M, b * a = c * a always implies b = c.

a. Power associativity
b. Quasifield
c. Magmas that are commutative but not associative
d. Cancellation property

16. In mathematics, an _____ is a statement about the relative size or order of two objects, or about whether they are the same or not

- The notation a < b means that a is less than b.
- The notation a > b means that a is greater than b.
- The notation a ≠ b means that a is not equal to b, but does not say that one is bigger than the other or even that they can be compared in size.

In all these cases, a is not equal to b, hence, '_____'.

These relations are known as strict _____

- The notation a ≤ b means that a is less than or equal to b;
- The notation a ≥ b means that a is greater than or equal to b;

An additional use of the notation is to show that one quantity is much greater than another, normally by several orders of magnitude.

- The notation a << b means that a is much less than b.
- The notation a >> b means that a is much greater than b.

If the sense of the _____ is the same for all values of the variables for which its members are defined, then the _____ is called an 'absolute' or 'unconditional' _____. If the sense of an _____ holds only for certain values of the variables involved, but is reversed or destroyed for other values of the variables, it is called a conditional _____.

An _____ may appear unsolvable because it only states whether a number is larger or smaller than another number; but it is possible to apply the same operations for equalities to inequalities. For example, to find x for the _____ 10x > 23 one would divide 23 by 10.

a. A chemical equation
b. A posteriori
c. A Mathematical Theory of Communication
d. Inequality

17. _____ is the likelihood or chance that something is the case or will happen. Theoretical _____ is used extensively in areas such as statistics, mathematics, science and philosophy to draw conclusions about the likelihood of potential events and the underlying mechanics of complex systems.

The word _____ does not have a consistent direct definition.

a. Discrete random variable
b. Probability
c. Standardized moment
d. Statistical significance

18. In mathematics, the _____ is a direct product of sets. The _____ is named after René Descartes, whose formulation of analytic geometry gave rise to this concept.

Specifically, the _____ of two sets X and Y, denoted X × Y, is the set of all possible ordered pairs whose first component is a member of X and whose second component is a member of Y:

$$X \times Y = \{(x,y) | x \in X \text{ and } y \in Y\}.$$

For example, the _____ of the 13-element set of standard playing card ranks {Ace, King, Queen, Jack, 10, 9, 8, 7, 6, 5, 4, 3, 2} and the four-element set of card suits {â™ , â™¥, â™¦, â™£} is the 52-element set of all possible playing cards ,, ...,,, ...,}.

a. Disjoint sets
b. Choice function
c. Set of all sets
d. Cartesian product

Chapter 8. INTEGERS

19. A _____, from the French patron, is a type of theme of recurring events of or objects, sometimes referred to as elements of a set. These elements repeat in a predictable manner. It can be a template or model which can be used to generate things or parts of a thing, especially if the things that are created have enough in common for the underlying _____ to be inferred, in which case the things are said to exhibit the unique _____.
   - a. 2-3 heap
   - b. Pattern
   - c. 1-center problem
   - d. 120-cell

20. In discrete mathematics and predominantly in set theory, a _____ is a concept used in comparisons of sets to refer to the unique values of one set in relation to another. The terms 'absolute' and 'relative' _____ refer to more specific applications of the concept, with universal _____s referring to elements unique to the universal set and the latter referring to the unique elements of one set in relation to another. In this image, the universal set is represented by the border of the image, and the set A as a disc.
   - a. Derivative algebra
   - b. Huge
   - c. Kernel
   - d. Complement

21. A _____ is a device for performing mathematical calculations, distinguished from a computer by having a limited problem solving ability and an interface optimized for interactive calculation rather than programming. _____s can be hardware or software, and mechanical or electronic, and are often built into devices such as PDAs or mobile phones.

Modern electronic _____s are generally small, digital, and usually inexpensive.

   - a. 2-3 heap
   - b. 1-center problem
   - c. 120-cell
   - d. Calculator

22. In mathematics, the _____ of a real number is its numerical value without regard to its sign. So, for example, 3 is the _____ of both 3 and −3.

The _____ of a number a is denoted by $|a|$.

Generalizations of the _____ for real numbers occur in a wide variety of mathematical settings.

   - a. A chemical equation
   - b. A Mathematical Theory of Communication
   - c. Absolute value
   - d. Area hyperbolic functions

23. In geometry, a _____ is defined as a quadrilateral where all four of its angles are right angles.
   - a. Cantor-Dedekind axiom
   - b. Point group in two dimensions
   - c. Polytope
   - d. Rectangle

24. In mathematics, computing, linguistics and related subjects, an _____ is a sequence of finite instructions, often used for calculation and data processing. It is formally a type of effective method in which a list of well-defined instructions for completing a task will, when given an initial state, proceed through a well-defined series of successive states, eventually terminating in an end-state. The transition from one state to the next is not necessarily deterministic; some _____s, known as probabilistic _____s, incorporate randomness.
   - a. Algorithm
   - b. Approximate counting algorithm
   - c. In-place algorithm
   - d. Out-of-core

25. _____ is the mathematical operation of scaling one number by another. It is one of the four basic operations in elementary arithmetic.

_____ is defined for whole numbers in terms of repeated addition; for example, 4 multiplied by 3 can be calculated by adding 3 copies of 4 together:

$$4 + 4 + 4 = 12.$$

_____ of rational numbers and real numbers is defined by systematic generalization of this basic idea.

a. Highest common factor
b. The number 0 is even.
c. Least common multiple
d. Multiplication

26. A _____ is an algorithm to multiply two numbers. Depending on the size of the numbers, different algorithms are in use. Efficient _____s have been around since the advent of the decimal system.
a. Spigot algorithm
b. Double dabble
c. Karatsuba algorithm
d. Multiplication algorithm

27. In mathematics, and in particular in abstract algebra, distributivity is a property of binary operations that generalises the _____ law from elementary algebra.
a. Closure with a twist
b. General linear group
c. Permutation
d. Distributive

28. In mathematics, a _____ of an integer n is an integer which evenly divides n without leaving a remainder.

For example, 7 is a _____ of 42 because 42/7 = 6. We also say 42 is divisible by 7 or 42 is a multiple of 7 or 7 divides 42 or 7 is a factor of 42 and we usually write 7 | 42.

a. 2-3 heap
b. 120-cell
c. 1-center problem
d. Divisor

29. In abstract algebra, a nonzero element a of a ring is a _____ if there exists a nonzero b such that ab = 0. Right zero divisors are defined analogously, that is, a nonzero element a of a ring is a right zero divisor if there exists a nonzero c such that ca = 0. An element that is both a left and a right zero divisor is simply called a zero divisor.
a. Restriction of scalars
b. Binary function
c. Linear combinations
d. Left zero divisor

30. In mathematics, a _____ can mean either an element of the set {1, 2, 3, ...} (i.e the positive integers) or an element of the set {0, 1, 2, 3, ...} (i.e. the non-negative integers).
a. FISH
b. Bounded
c. Degrees of freedom
d. Whole number

31. Exponentiation is a mathematical operation, written a^n, involving two numbers, the base a and the _____ n. When n is a positive integer, exponentiation corresponds to repeated multiplication:

Chapter 8. INTEGERS

$$a^n = \underbrace{a \times \cdots \times a}_{n},$$

just as multiplication by a positive integer corresponds to repeated addition:

$$a \times n = \underbrace{a + \cdots + a}_{n}.$$

The _____ is usually shown as a superscript to the right of the base. The exponentiation a^n can be read as: a raised to the n-th power, a raised to the power [of] n or possibly a raised to the _____ [of] n, or more briefly: a to the n-th power or a to the power [of] n, or even more briefly: a to the n.

- a. Exponential tree
- b. Exponential sum
- c. Exponentiating by squaring
- d. Exponent

32. In mathematics, the _____ of a ring R, often denoted cha, is defined to be the smallest number of times one must add the ring's multiplicative identity element to itself to get the additive identity element; the ring is said to have _____ zero if this repeated sum never reaches the additive identity. That is, cha is the smallest positive number n such that

$$\underbrace{1 + \cdots + 1}_{n \text{ summands}} = 0$$

if such a number n exists, and 0 otherwise. The _____ may also be taken to be the exponent of the ring's additive group, that is, the smallest positive n such that

$$\underbrace{a + \cdots + a}_{n \text{ summands}} = 0$$

for every element a of the ring.

- a. Disk
- b. Characteristic
- c. Coherent
- d. Class

33. _____, also sometimes known as standard form or as exponential notation, is a way of writing numbers that accommodates values too large or small to be conveniently written in standard decimal notation. _____ has a number of useful properties and is often favored by scientists, mathematicians and engineers, who work with such numbers.

In _____, numbers are written in the form:

$$a \times 10^b$$

a. 1-center problem
b. Leading zero
c. Radix point
d. Scientific notation

34. In a positional numeral system, the decimal separator is a symbol used to mark the boundary between the integral and the fractional parts of a decimal numeral. When used in context of Arabic numerals, terms implying the symbol used are _____ and decimal comma.

The decimal separator is mathematically a radix point.

a. Fibonacci coding
b. Hexadecimal
c. Decimal point
d. Tetradecimal

35. In mathematics, a _____ is a number which can be expressed as a ratio of two integers. Non-integer _____s are usually written as the vulgar fraction $\frac{a}{b}$, where b is not zero. a is called the numerator, and b the denominator.

a. Tally marks
b. Minkowski distance
c. Pre-algebra
d. Rational number

Chapter 9. RATIONAL NUMBERS AND REAL NUMBERS, WITH AN INTRODUCTION TO ALGEBRA

1. In mathematics, an _____ or member of a set is any one of the distinct objects that make up that set.

Writing A = {1,2,3,4}, means that the _____s of the set A are the numbers 1, 2, 3 and 4. Groups of _____s of A, for example {1,2}, are subsets of A.

    a. Universal code
    c. Order
    b. Element
    d. Ideal

2. In game theory, a player's _____ in a game is a complete plan of action for whatever situation might arise; this fully determines the player's behaviour. A player's _____ will determine the action the player will take at any stage of the game, for every possible history of play up to that stage.

A _____ profile is a set of strategies for each player which fully specifies all actions in a game.

    a. Correlated equilibrium
    c. Sir Philip Sidney game
    b. Matching pennies
    d. Strategy

3. _____ is a special mathematical relationship between two quantities.Two quantities are called proportional if they vary in such a way that one of the quantities is a constant multiple of the other, or equivalently if they have a constant ratio.
    a. Compression
    c. Depth
    b. Proportionality
    d. Discontinuity

4. In mathematics, a _____ is a number which can be expressed as a ratio of two integers. Non-integer _____s are usually written as the vulgar fraction $\frac{a}{b}$, where b is not zero. a is called the numerator, and b the denominator.
    a. Tally marks
    c. Rational number
    b. Pre-algebra
    d. Minkowski distance

5. In mathematics, the _____s may be described informally in several different ways. The _____s include both rational numbers, such as 42 and −23/129, and irrational numbers, such as pi and the square root of two; or, a _____ can be given by an infinite decimal representation, such as 2.4871773339...., where the digits continue in some way; or, the _____s may be thought of as points on an infinitely long number line.

These descriptions of the _____s, while intuitively accessible, are not sufficiently rigorous for the purposes of pure mathematics.

    a. Minkowski distance
    c. Real number
    b. Pre-algebra
    d. Tally marks

6. The _____ are the set of numbers consisting of the natural numbers including 0 and their negatives. They are numbers that can be written without a fractional or decimal component, and fall within the set {... −2, −1, 0, 1, 2, ...}.
    a. A chemical equation
    c. A Mathematical Theory of Communication
    b. A posteriori
    d. Integers

7. In mathematics, _____ and undefined are used to explain whether or not expressions have meaningful, sensible, and unambiguous values. Not all branches of mathematics come to the same conclusion.

Chapter 9. RATIONAL NUMBERS AND REAL NUMBERS, WITH AN INTRODUCTION TO ALGEBRA

The following expressions are undefined in all contexts, but remarks in the analysis section may apply.

a. Plugging in
b. Toy model
c. Defined
d. LHS

8. In mathematics, hyperbolic n-space, denoted H^n, is the maximally symmetric, simply connected, n-dimensional Riemannian manifold with constant sectional curvature −1. _____ is the principal example of a space exhibiting hyperbolic geometry. It can be thought of as the negative-curvature analogue of the n-sphere.

a. Hyperbolic geometry
b. Horocycle
c. Margulis lemma
d. Hyperbolic space

9. An _____ is a number which is involved in addition. A number being added is considered to be an _____.

a. A Mathematical Theory of Communication
b. A chemical equation
c. Addend
d. A posteriori

10. In mathematics, a _____ is a picture of a straight line in which the integers are shown as specially-marked points evenly spaced on the line. Although this image only shows the integers from -9 to 9, the line includes all real numbers, continuing 'forever' in each direction. It is often used as an aid in teaching simple addition and subtraction, especially involving negative numbers.

a. Real number
b. Number system
c. Point plotting
d. Number line

11. In mathematics the _____ of a set which is equipped with the operation of addition is an element which, when added to any element x in the set, yields x. One of the most familiar additive identities is the number 0 from elementary mathematics, but additive identities occur in other mathematical structures where addition is defined, such as in groups and rings.

- The _____ familiar from elementary mathematics is zero, denoted 0. For example,

$5 + 0 = 5 = 0 + 5.$

- In the natural numbers N and all of its supersets, the _____ is 0. Thus for any one of these numbers n,

$n + 0 = n = 0 + n.$

Let N be a set which is closed under the operation of addition, denoted +. An _____ for N is any element e such that for any element n in N,

$e + n = n = n + e.$

a. Algebraically independent
b. Unit ring
c. Additive identity
d. Unique factorization domain

12. In mathematics, the _____ of a number n is the number that, when added to n, yields zero. The _____ of n is denoted −n. For example, 7 is −7, because 7 + (−7) = 0, and the _____ of −0.3 is 0.3, because −0.3 + 0.3 = 0.

Chapter 9. RATIONAL NUMBERS AND REAL NUMBERS, WITH AN INTRODUCTION TO ALGEBRA

a. Arity
b. Associativity
c. Algebraic structure
d. Additive inverse

13. In mathematics, a set is said to be _____ if the operation on members of the set produces a member of the set. For example, the real numbers are closed under subtraction, but the natural numbers are not: 3 and 7 are both natural numbers, but the result of 3 − 7 is not.

Similarly, a set is said to be closed under a collection of operations if it is closed under each of the operations individually.

a. Closed under some operation
b. Continuous linear extension
c. Control chart
d. Contingency table

14. The _____ is a rule which states that when you add or multiply numbers, changing the order doesn't change the result.

a. Semigroupoid
b. Conditional event algebra
c. Coimage
d. Commutative law

15. In mathematics, the term _____ has several different important meanings:

- An _____ is an equality that remains true regardless of the values of any variables that appear within it, to distinguish it from an equality which is true under more particular conditions. For this, the 'triple bar' symbol ≡ is sometimes used.
- In algebra, an _____ or _____ element of a set S with a binary operation · is an element e that, when combined with any element x of S, produces that same x. That is, e·x = x·e = x for all x in S.
  - The _____ function from a set S to itself, often denoted id or id_S, s the function such that i = x for all x in S. This function serves as the _____ element in the set of all functions from S to itself with respect to function composition.
  - In linear algebra, the _____ matrix of size n is the n-by-n square matrix with ones on the main diagonal and zeros elsewhere. This matrix serves as the _____ with respect to matrix multiplication.

A common example of the first meaning is the trigonometric _____

$$\sin^2 \theta + \cos^2 \theta = 1$$

which is true for all real values of θ, as opposed to

$$\cos \theta = 1,$$

which is true only for some values of θ, not all. For example, the latter equation is true when $\theta = 0$, false when $\theta = 2$

Chapter 9. RATIONAL NUMBERS AND REAL NUMBERS, WITH AN INTRODUCTION TO ALGEBRA

The concepts of 'additive _____' and 'multiplicative _____' are central to the Peano axioms. The number 0 is the 'additive _____' for integers, real numbers, and complex numbers. For the real numbers, for all $a \in \mathbb{R}$,

$$0 + a = a,$$

$$a + 0 = a, \text{ and}$$

$$0 + 0 = 0.$$

Similarly, The number 1 is the 'multiplicative _____' for integers, real numbers, and complex numbers.

- a. Identity
- b. Action
- c. ARIA
- d. Intersection

16. In mathematics, _____ is a property that a binary operation can have. It means that, within an expression containing two or more of the same associative operators in a row, the order that the operations are performed does not matter as long as the sequence of the operands is not changed. That is, rearranging the parentheses in such an expression will not change its value.
- a. Associativity
- b. Unital
- c. Algebraically closed
- d. Idempotence

17. _____ is the likelihood or chance that something is the case or will happen. Theoretical _____ is used extensively in areas such as statistics, mathematics, science and philosophy to draw conclusions about the likelihood of potential events and the underlying mechanics of complex systems.

The word _____ does not have a consistent direct definition.

- a. Standardized moment
- b. Discrete random variable
- c. Statistical significance
- d. Probability

18. In mathematics, the _____ or least common denominator is the least common multiple of the denominators of a set of vulgar fractions. It is the smallest positive integer that is a multiple of the denominators. For instance, the _____ of

$$\left\{ \frac{5}{12}, \frac{11}{18} \right\}$$

is 36 because the least common multiple of 12 and 18 is 36.

- a. The number 0 is even.
- b. Subtrahend
- c. Lowest common denominator
- d. Highest common factor

19. In mathematics, the notion of cancellative is a generalization of the notion of invertible.

Chapter 9. RATIONAL NUMBERS AND REAL NUMBERS, WITH AN INTRODUCTION TO ALGEBRA

An element a in a magma has the left _____ if for all b and c in M, a * b = a * c always implies b = c.

An element a in a magma has the right _____ if for all b and c in M, b * a = c * a always implies b = c.

a. Magmas that are commutative but not associative
b. Quasifield
c. Power associativity
d. Cancellation property

20. In discrete mathematics and predominantly in set theory, a _____ is a concept used in comparisons of sets to refer to the unique values of one set in relation to another. The terms 'absolute' and 'relative' _____ refer to more specific applications of the concept, with universal _____s referring to elements unique to the universal set and the latter referring to the unique elements of one set in relation to another. In this image, the universal set is represented by the border of the image, and the set A as a disc.

a. Derivative algebra
b. Huge
c. Complement
d. Kernel

21. In mathematics, computing, linguistics and related subjects, an _____ is a sequence of finite instructions, often used for calculation and data processing. It is formally a type of effective method in which a list of well-defined instructions for completing a task will, when given an initial state, proceed through a well-defined series of successive states, eventually terminating in an end-state. The transition from one state to the next is not necessarily deterministic; some _____s, known as probabilistic _____s, incorporate randomness.

a. In-place algorithm
b. Out-of-core
c. Algorithm
d. Approximate counting algorithm

22. A _____ is a device for performing mathematical calculations, distinguished from a computer by having a limited problem solving ability and an interface optimized for interactive calculation rather than programming. _____s can be hardware or software, and mechanical or electronic, and are often built into devices such as PDAs or mobile phones.

Modern electronic _____s are generally small, digital, and usually inexpensive.

a. 120-cell
b. 1-center problem
c. 2-3 heap
d. Calculator

23. _____ is the mathematical operation of scaling one number by another. It is one of the four basic operations in elementary arithmetic.

_____ is defined for whole numbers in terms of repeated addition; for example, 4 multiplied by 3 can be calculated by adding 3 copies of 4 together:

$$4 + 4 + 4 = 12.$$

_____ of rational numbers and real numbers is defined by systematic generalization of this basic idea.

a. The number 0 is even.
b. Multiplication
c. Least common multiple
d. Highest common factor

Chapter 9. RATIONAL NUMBERS AND REAL NUMBERS, WITH AN INTRODUCTION TO ALGEBRA

24. In mathematics, the _____ is a direct product of sets. The _____ is named after René Descartes, whose formulation of analytic geometry gave rise to this concept.

Specifically, the _____ of two sets X and Y, denoted X × Y, is the set of all possible ordered pairs whose first component is a member of X and whose second component is a member of Y:

$$X \times Y = \{(x,y) | x \in X \text{ and } y \in Y\}.$$

For example, the _____ of the 13-element set of standard playing card ranks {Ace, King, Queen, Jack, 10, 9, 8, 7, 6, 5, 4, 3, 2} and the four-element set of card suits {â™ , â™¥, â™¦, â™£} is the 52-element set of all possible playing cards ,, ...,, ...,}.

a. Disjoint sets
b. Cartesian product
c. Choice function
d. Set of all sets

25. In mathematics, and in particular in abstract algebra, distributivity is a property of binary operations that generalises the _____ law from elementary algebra.

a. General linear group
b. Permutation
c. Closure with a twist
d. Distributive

26. A _____ is an algorithm to multiply two numbers. Depending on the size of the numbers, different algorithms are in use. Efficient _____s have been around since the advent of the decimal system.

a. Karatsuba algorithm
b. Spigot algorithm
c. Double dabble
d. Multiplication algorithm

27. In mathematics, a _____ for a number x, denoted by $\frac{1}{x}$ or x^{-1}, is a number which when multiplied by x yields the multiplicative identity, 1. The _____ of x is also called the reciprocal of x. The _____ of a fraction p/q is q/p.

a. Double exponential
b. Golden function
c. Hyperbolic function
d. Multiplicative inverse

28. In mathematics, the multiplicative inverse of a number x, denoted 1/x or x^{-1}, is the number which, when multiplied by x, yields 1. The multiplicative inverse of x is also called the _____ of x.

a. 1-center problem
b. 2-3 heap
c. 120-cell
d. Reciprocal

29. In mathematics, a _____ of an integer n is an integer which evenly divides n without leaving a remainder.

For example, 7 is a _____ of 42 because 42/7 = 6. We also say 42 is divisible by 7 or 42 is a multiple of 7 or 7 divides 42 or 7 is a factor of 42 and we usually write 7 | 42.

a. Divisor
b. 1-center problem
c. 120-cell
d. 2-3 heap

30. In mathematics, a _____ can mean either an element of the set {1, 2, 3, ...} (i.e the positive integers) or an element of the set {0, 1, 2, 3, ...} (i.e. the non-negative integers).

Chapter 9. RATIONAL NUMBERS AND REAL NUMBERS, WITH AN INTRODUCTION TO ALGEBRA

a. FISH
b. Degrees of freedom
c. Bounded
d. Whole number

31. The _____ of a material is defined as its mass per unit volume:

$$\rho = \frac{m}{V}$$

Different materials usually have different densities, so _____ is an important concept regarding buoyancy, metal purity and packaging.

In some cases _____ is expressed as the dimensionless quantities specific gravity or relative _____, in which case it is expressed in multiples of the _____ of some other standard material, usually water or air.

In a well-known story, Archimedes was given the task of determining whether King Hiero's goldsmith was embezzling gold during the manufacture of a wreath dedicated to the gods and replacing it with another, cheaper alloy.

a. 1-center problem
b. 2-3 heap
c. 120-cell
d. Density

32. In mathematics, an _____ is a statement about the relative size or order of two objects, or about whether they are the same or not

- The notation a < b means that a is less than b.
- The notation a > b means that a is greater than b.
- The notation a ≠ b means that a is not equal to b, but does not say that one is bigger than the other or even that they can be compared in size.

In all these cases, a is not equal to b, hence, '_____'.

These relations are known as strict _____

- The notation a ≤ b means that a is less than or equal to b;
- The notation a ≥ b means that a is greater than or equal to b;

An additional use of the notation is to show that one quantity is much greater than another, normally by several orders of magnitude.

- The notation a << b means that a is much less than b.
- The notation a >> b means that a is much greater than b.

Chapter 9. RATIONAL NUMBERS AND REAL NUMBERS, WITH AN INTRODUCTION TO ALGEBRA

If the sense of the _____ is the same for all values of the variables for which its members are defined, then the _____ is called an 'absolute' or 'unconditional' _____. If the sense of an _____ holds only for certain values of the variables involved, but is reversed or destroyed for other values of the variables, it is called a conditional _____.

An _____ may appear unsolvable because it only states whether a number is larger or smaller than another number; but it is possible to apply the same operations for equalities to inequalities. For example, to find x for the _____ 10x > 23 one would divide 23 by 10.

a. A posteriori
b. A chemical equation
c. Inequality
d. A Mathematical Theory of Communication

33. A _____ consists of three positive integers a, b, and c, such that $a^2 + b^2 = c^2$. Such a triple is commonly written, and a well-known example is. If is a _____, then so is for any positive integer k.

a. 120-cell
b. Pythagorean triple
c. 1-center problem
d. 2-3 heap

34. In mathematics, a _____ of a number x is a number r such that $r^2 = x$, or, in other words, a number r whose square is x. Every non-negative real number x has a unique non-negative _____, called the principal _____, which is denoted with a radical symbol as $\sqrt{x}$, or, using exponent notation, as $x^{1/2}$. For example, the principal _____ of 9 is 3, denoted $\sqrt{9} = 3$, because $3^2 = 3 \times 3 = 9$.

a. Square root
b. Hyperbolic functions
c. Double exponential
d. Multiplicative inverse

35. In vascular plants, the _____ is the organ of a plant body that typically lies below the surface of the soil. This is not always the case, however, since a _____ can also be aerial (that is, growing above the ground) or aerating (that is, growing up above the ground or especially above water.) Furthermore, a stem normally occurring below ground is not exceptional either

a. 1-center problem
b. 120-cell
c. 2-3 heap
d. Root

36. In general, an object is complete if nothing needs to be added to it. This notion is made more specific in various fields.

In logic, semantic _____ is the converse of soundness for formal systems.

a. Giuseppe Peano
b. Completeness
c. Set theory
d. Logical equality

37. Exponentiation is a mathematical operation, written a^n, involving two numbers, the base a and the _____ n. When n is a positive integer, exponentiation corresponds to repeated multiplication:

$$a^n = \underbrace{a \times \cdots \times a}_{n},$$

Chapter 9. RATIONAL NUMBERS AND REAL NUMBERS, WITH AN INTRODUCTION TO ALGEBRA

just as multiplication by a positive integer corresponds to repeated addition:

$$a \times n = \underbrace{a + \cdots + a}_{n}.$$

The _____ is usually shown as a superscript to the right of the base. The exponentiation a^n can be read as: a raised to the n-th power, a raised to the power [of] n or possibly a raised to the _____ [of] n, or more briefly: a to the n-th power or a to the power [of] n, or even more briefly: a to the n.

a. Exponentiating by squaring
b. Exponential sum
c. Exponential tree
d. Exponent

38. In mathematics, an algebraic group G contains a unique maximal normal solvable subgroup; and this subgroup is closed. Its identity component is called the _____ of G.
   a. Composite
   b. Barycentric coordinates
   c. Block size
   d. Radical

39. In a positional numeral system, the decimal separator is a symbol used to mark the boundary between the integral and the fractional parts of a decimal numeral. When used in context of Arabic numerals, terms implying the symbol used are _____ and decimal comma.

The decimal separator is mathematically a radix point.

   a. Decimal point
   b. Hexadecimal
   c. Tetradecimal
   d. Fibonacci coding

40. In mathematics, a _____ is a constant multiplicative factor of a certain object. For example, in the expression $9x^2$, the _____ of x^2 is 9.

The object can be such things as a variable, a vector, a function, etc.

   a. Coefficient
   b. Multivariate division algorithm
   c. Stability radius
   d. Fibonacci polynomials

41. In mathematics, a _____ of a set X is a collection of sets such that X is a subset of the union of sets in the collection. In symbols, if

$$C = \{U_\alpha : \alpha \in A\}$$

Chapter 9. RATIONAL NUMBERS AND REAL NUMBERS, WITH AN INTRODUCTION TO ALGEBRA

is an indexed family of sets U_α, then C is a _____ of X if

$$X \subseteq \bigcup_{\alpha \in A} U_\alpha$$

_____s are commonly used in the context of topology. If the set X is a topological space, then a _____ C of X is a collection of subsets U_α of X whose union is the whole space X.

a. Manifold
b. Cover
c. Generalised metric
d. Contractible space

42. A _____ is a 2D geometric symbolic representation of information according to some visualization technique. Sometimes, the technique uses a 3D visualization which is then projected onto the 2D surface. The word graph is sometimes used as a synonym for _____.
a. 2-3 heap
b. Diagram
c. 1-center problem
d. 120-cell

43. In mathematics, the _____ or Pythagoras' theorem is a relation in Euclidean geometry among the three sides of a right triangle. The theorem is named after the Greek mathematician Pythagoras, who by tradition is credited with its discovery and proof, although it is often argued that knowledge of the theory predates him.. The theorem is as follows:

In any right triangle, the area of the square whose side is the hypotenuse is equal to the sum of the areas of the squares whose sides are the two legs.

a. 120-cell
b. 2-3 heap
c. 1-center problem
d. Pythagorean theorem

44. In mathematics, a _____ is a statement that can be proved on the basis of explicitly stated or previously agreed assumptions.
a. Boolean function
b. Theorem
c. Logical value
d. Disjunction introduction

45. In mathematics and computer science, _____ (also base-16, hexa or base, of 16. It uses sixteen distinct symbols, most often the symbols 0-9 to represent values zero to nine, and A, B, C, D, E, F (or a through f) to represent values ten to fifteen.

Its primary use is as a human friendly representation of binary coded values, so it is often used in digital electronics and computer engineering.

a. Tetradecimal
b. Factoradic
c. Radix
d. Hexadecimal

46. The x-axis is the horizontal axis of a two- dimensional plot in the _____, that is typically pointed to the right. Also known as a right-handed coordinate system.

Chapter 9. RATIONAL NUMBERS AND REAL NUMBERS, WITH AN INTRODUCTION TO ALGEBRA

a. 2-3 heap
b. Cartesian coordinate system
c. 1-center problem
d. 120-cell

47. Leonardo of Pisa (c. 1170 - c. 1250), also known as Leonardo Pisano, Leonardo Bonacci, Leonardo _____, or, most commonly, simply _____, was an Italian mathematician, considered by some 'the most talented mathematician of the Middle Ages'.
a. Harry Hinsley
b. Guido Castelnuovo
c. Ralph C. Merkle
d. Fibonacci

48. The mathematical concept of a _____ expresses the intuitive idea of deterministic dependence between two quantities, one of which is viewed as primary and the other as secondary. A _____ then is a way to associate a unique output for each input of a specified type, for example, a real number or an element of a given set.
a. Grill
b. Function
c. Coherent
d. Going up

49. In mathematics, the _____ of a Euclidean space is a special point, usually denoted by the letter O, used as a fixed point of reference for the geometry of the surrounding space. In a Cartesian coordinate system, the _____ is the point where the axes of the system intersect. In Euclidean geometry, the _____ may be chosen freely as any convenient point of reference.
a. OMAC
b. Interval
c. Autonomous system
d. Origin

50. The _____ is the horizontal axis of a two- dimensional plot in the Cartesian coordinate system, that is typically pointed to the right. Also known as a right-handed coordinate system.
a. 1-center problem
b. 2-3 heap
c. 120-cell
d. X-axis

51. The _____ is one of the coordinates of a point in a two or three-dimensional cartesian coordinate system, equal to the distance of a point from the y-axis in a 2D system, or from the plane of y and z axes in a 3D system, measured along a line parallel to the x axis.
a. 1-center problem
b. 120-cell
c. X-coordinate
d. 2-3 heap

52. In reference to a 2D and 3D plane, the _____ is the vertical height of a 2D or 3D object.
a. 2-3 heap
b. 1-center problem
c. 120-cell
d. Y-axis

53. The _____ is the distance between a point and an axis in the Cartesian Coordinate System.
a. 2-3 heap
b. Y-coordinate
c. 1-center problem
d. 120-cell

54. A _____ consists of one quarter of the coordinate plane.
a. 120-cell
b. 2-3 heap
c. 1-center problem
d. Quadrant

Chapter 9. RATIONAL NUMBERS AND REAL NUMBERS, WITH AN INTRODUCTION TO ALGEBRA

55. In abstract algebra, a field extension L /K is called _____ if every element of L is _____ over K. Field extensions which are not _____.

For example, the field extension R/Q, that is the field of real numbers as an extension of the field of rational numbers, is transcendental, while the field extensions C/R and Q

- a. Echo
- b. Identity
- c. Algebraic
- d. Ideal

56. In mathematics, a homogeneous polynomial is a polynomial whose terms all have the same total degree. For example, x^5 + $2x^3y^2$ + $9x^1y^4$ is a homogeneous polynomial of degree 5, in two variables; the sum of the exponents in each term is always 5. An _____, or simply form, is another name for a homogeneous polynomial.

- a. A Mathematical Theory of Communication
- b. A chemical equation
- c. A posteriori
- d. Algebraic form

57. A _____, in mathematics, is a polynomial function of the form $f(x) = ax^2 + bx + c$, where $a \neq 0$. The graph of a _____ is a parabola whose major axis is parallel to the y-axis.

The expression $ax^2 + bx + c$ in the definition of a _____ is a polynomial of degree 2 or a 2nd degree polynomial, because the highest exponent of x is 2.

- a. Multivariate division algorithm
- b. Discriminant
- c. Laguerre polynomials
- d. Quadratic function

58. The _____ is a function in mathematics. The application of this function to a value x is written as ex. Equivalently, this can be written in the form e^x, where e is a mathematical constant, the base of the natural logarithm, which equals approximately 2.718281828, and is also known as Euler's number.

- a. A Mathematical Theory of Communication
- b. Exponential function
- c. Area hyperbolic functions
- d. A chemical equation

59. _____ is the process in which an unstable atomic nucleus loses energy by emitting ionizing particles and radiation. This decay, or loss of energy, results in an atom of one type, called the parent nuclide transforming to an atom of a different type, called the daughter nuclide. For example: a carbon-14 atom emits radiation and transforms to a nitrogen-14 atom.

- a. 1-center problem
- b. Radioactive decay
- c. Half-life
- d. 120-cell

60. In mathematics, a _____ is a function of the form

f3 + bx^2 + cx + d,

where a is nonzero; or in other words, a polynomial of degree three. The derivative of a _____ is a quadratic function. The integral of a _____ is a quartic function.

Chapter 9. RATIONAL NUMBERS AND REAL NUMBERS, WITH AN INTRODUCTION TO ALGEBRA

a. Quadratic equation
c. Cubic function
b. Linear equation
d. Quartic equation

61. The _____ principle is a form of technical analysis that attempts to forecast trends in the financial markets and other collective activities. It is named after Ralph Nelson Elliott, an accountant who developed the concept in the 1930s: he proposed that market prices unfold in specific patterns, which practitioners today call _____s. Elliott published his views of market behavior in the book The Wave Principle, in a series of articles in Financial World magazine in 1939, and most fully in his final major work, Nature's Laws - The Secret of the Universe.

a. A Mathematical Theory of Communication
c. A posteriori
b. A chemical equation
d. Elliott wave

62. The word _____ has many distinct meanings in different fields of knowledge, depending on their methodologies and the context of discussion. Broadly speaking we can say that a _____ is some kind of belief or claim that (supposedly) explains, asserts, or consolidates some class of claims. Additionally, in contrast with a theorem the statement of the _____ is generally accepted only in some tentative fashion as opposed to regarding it as having been conclusively established.

a. Per mil
c. Transport of structure
b. Defined
d. Theory

63. The _____ , is achieved in a packed stadium when successive groups of spectators briefly stand and raise their arms. Each spectator is required to rise at the same time as those straight in front and behind, and slightly after the person immediately to either the right or the left. Immediately upon stretching to full height, the spectator returns to the usual seated position.

a. Thermodynamic limit
c. Pauli exclusion principle
b. Wave
d. Lagrangian

Chapter 10. STATISTICS

1. A _____ is the result of applying a function to a set of data.

More formally, statistical theory defines a _____ as a function of a sample where the function itself is independent of the sample's distribution: the term is used both for the function and for the value of the function on a given sample.

A _____ is distinct from an unknown statistical parameter, which is not computable from a sample.

- a. Spatial dependence
- b. Loss function
- c. Parameter space
- d. Statistic

2. _____ is a mathematical science pertaining to the collection, analysis, interpretation or explanation, and presentation of data. It also provides tools for prediction and forecasting based on data. It is applicable to a wide variety of academic disciplines, from the natural and social sciences to the humanities, government and business.

- a. Regression toward the mean
- b. Probability distribution
- c. Statistics
- d. Percentile rank

3. In mathematics and in the sciences, a _____ (plural: _____e, formulæ or _____s) is a concise way of expressing information symbolically (as in a mathematical or chemical _____), or a general relationship between quantities. One of many famous _____e is Albert Einstein's $E = mc^2$ (see special relativity)

In mathematics, a _____ is a key to solve an equation with variables. For example, the problem of determining the volume of a sphere is one that requires a significant amount of integral calculus to solve.

- a. 1-center problem
- b. Formula
- c. 2-3 heap
- d. 120-cell

4. In game theory, a player's _____ in a game is a complete plan of action for whatever situation might arise; this fully determines the player's behaviour. A player's _____ will determine the action the player will take at any stage of the game, for every possible history of play up to that stage.

A _____ profile is a set of strategies for each player which fully specifies all actions in a game.

- a. Correlated equilibrium
- b. Sir Philip Sidney game
- c. Strategy
- d. Matching pennies

5. A _____ plot is a graphical method that allows the comparison of two biological sequences and identify regions of close similarity between them. It is a kind of recurrence plot.

The simplest way to visualize the similarity between two protein sequences is to use a similarity matrix, known as a _____.

- a. Duality
- b. Clipping
- c. Constructivism
- d. Dot plot

Chapter 10. STATISTICS

6. A _____ is is a graphical technique for presenting a data set drawn by hand or produced by a mechanical or electronic plotter. It is a graph depicting the relationship between two or more variables used, for instance, in visualising scientific data.

_____s play an important role in statistics and data analysis.

a. Lattice
b. C-35
c. Dini
d. Plot

7. In statistics the _____ of an event i is the number n_i of times the event occurred in the experiment or the study. These frequencies are often graphically represented in histograms.

We speak of absolute frequencies, when the counts n_i themselves are given and of

$$f_i = \frac{n_i}{N} = \frac{n_i}{\sum_i n_i}$$

Taking the f_i for all i and tabulating or plotting them leads to a _____ distribution.

a. Digital room correction
b. Subharmonic
c. Frequency
d. Robinson-Dadson curves

8. In botany, a _____ is an above-ground plant organ specialized for photosynthesis. For this purpose, a _____ is typically flat and thin, to expose the cells containing chloroplast to light over a broad area, and to allow light to penetrate fully into the tissues. Leaves are also the sites in most plants where transpiration and guttation take place.

a. 2-3 heap
b. 120-cell
c. 1-center problem
d. Leaf

9. A bar chart or _____ is a chart with rectangular bars with lengths proportional to the values that they represent. Bar charts are used for comparing two or more values. The bars can be horizontally or vertically oriented.

a. 2-3 heap
b. Bar graph
c. 1-center problem
d. 120-cell

10. In statistics, a _____ is a graphical display of tabulated frequencies, shown as bars. It shows what proportion of cases fall into each of several categories. A _____ differs from a bar chart in that it is the area of the bar that denotes the value, not the height as in bar charts, a crucial distinction when the categories are not of uniform width.

a. Probability distribution
b. Histogram
c. First-hitting-time models
d. Standardized moment

11. In a graph theory, the _____ L

One of the earliest and most important theorems about _____s is due to Hassler Whitney, who proved that with one exceptional case the structure of G can be recovered completely from its _____.

a. Vertex-transitive graph
c. Sparse graph
b. Line graph
d. Bivariegated graph

12. A _____ is a simple shape of Euclidean geometry consisting of those points in a plane which are at a constant distance, called the radius, from a fixed point, called the center. A _____ with center A is sometimes denoted by the symbol A.

A chord of a _____ is a line segment whose two endpoints lie on the _____.

a. Circumcircle
c. Circle
b. Circular segment
d. Malfatti circles

13. In graph theory, a _____ is a graph whose vertices can be associated with chords of a circle such that two vertices are adjacent if and only if the corresponding chords in the circle intersect.

Spinrad (1994) gives an $O(n^2)$-time recognition algorithm for _____s that also computes a circle model of the input graph if it is a _____.

A number of other problems that are NP-complete on general graphs have polynomial time algorithms when restricted to _____s.

a. Planar graph
c. Sparse graph
b. Circle Graph
d. Vertex-transitive graph

14. _____ or pictograph is a symbol representing a concept, object, activity, place or event by illustration. Pictography is a form of writing in which ideas are transmitted through drawing. It is a basis of cuneiform and, to some extent, hieroglyphic writing, which uses drawings also as phonetic letters or determinative rhymes.

a. Pictographs
c. Treemapping
b. Sparkline
d. Pictogram

15. _____ are symbols representing a concept, object, activity, place or event by illustration.

a. Sparkline
c. Treemapping
b. Pictogram
d. Pictographs

16. In probability theory and statistics, _____ indicates the strength and direction of a linear relationship between two random variables. That is in contrast with the usage of the term in colloquial speech, denoting any relationship, not necessarily linear. In general statistical usage, _____ or co-relation refers to the departure of two random variables from independence.

a. Summary statistics
c. Random variables
b. Sample size
d. Correlation

17. In statistics, an _____ is an observation that is numerically distant from the rest of the data. Statistics derived from data sets that include _____s may be misleading. For example, if one is calculating the average temperature of 10 objects in a room, and most are between 20 and 25 degrees Celsius, but an oven is at 175 °C, the median of the data may be 23 °C but the mean temperature will be between 35.5 and 40 °C.

Chapter 10. STATISTICS

a. A Mathematical Theory of Communication
b. Outlier
c. A posteriori
d. A chemical equation

18. The _____ fallacy is an informal fallacy. It ascribes cause where none exists. The flaw is failing to account for natural fluctuations.
   a. Differential
   b. Degrees of freedom
   c. Regression
   d. Depth

19. In mathematics, an _____, or central tendency of a data set refers to a measure of the 'middle' or 'expected' value of the data set. There are many different descriptive statistics that can be chosen as a measurement of the central tendency of the data items.

An _____ is a single value that is meant to typify a list of values.

   a. A chemical equation
   b. A posteriori
   c. Average
   d. A Mathematical Theory of Communication

20. In mathematics, an average, or _____ of a data set refers to a measure of the 'middle' or 'expected' value of the data set. There are many different descriptive statistics that can be chosen as a measurement of the _____ of the data items.

An average is a single value that is meant to typify a list of values.

   a. Trimean
   b. Mean reciprocal rank
   c. Quartile
   d. Central tendency

21. In mathematics the concept of a _____ generalizes notions such as 'length', 'area', and 'volume'. Informally, given some base set, a '_____' is any consistent assignment of 'sizes' to the subsets of the base set. Depending on the application, the 'size' of a subset may be interpreted as its physical size, the amount of something that lies within the subset, or the probability that some random process will yield a result within the subset.
   a. Congruent
   b. Measure
   c. Cusp
   d. Lattice

22. In geometry, a _____ of a triangle is a line segment joining a vertex to the midpoint of the opposing side. Every triangle has exactly three _____s; one running from each vertex to the opposite side.

The three _____s are concurrent at a point known as the triangle's centroid, or center of mass of the triangle.

   a. Statistical significance
   b. Percentile rank
   c. Correlation
   d. Median

23. In statistics, the _____ is the value that occurs the most frequently in a data set or a probability distribution. In some fields, notably education, sample data are often called scores, and the sample _____ is known as the modal score.

Like the statistical mean and the median, the _____ is a way of capturing important information about a random variable or a population in a single quantity.

a. Deltoid
b. Field
c. Function
d. Mode

24. In geometry and trigonometry, an _____ is the figure formed by two rays sharing a common endpoint, called the vertex of the _____. The magnitude of the _____ is the 'amount of rotation' that separates the two rays, and can be measured by considering the length of circular arc swept out when one ray is rotated about the vertex to coincide with the other. Where there is no possibility of confusion, the term '_____' is used interchangeably for both the geometric configuration itself and for its angular magnitude.

a. A chemical equation
b. A posteriori
c. A Mathematical Theory of Communication
d. Angle

25. In statistics, _____ has two related meanings:

- the arithmetic _____.
- the expected value of a random variable, which is also called the population _____.

It is sometimes stated that the '_____' _____s average. This is incorrect if '_____' is taken in the specific sense of 'arithmetic _____' as there are different types of averages: the _____, median, and mode. For instance, average house prices almost always use the median value for the average.

For a real-valued random variable X, the _____ is the expectation of X.

a. Mean
b. Statistical population
c. Proportional hazards model
d. Probability

26. In mathematics and statistics, the _____ of a list of numbers is the sum of all of the list divided by the number of items in the list. If the list is a statistical population, then the mean of that population is called a population mean. If the list is a statistical sample, we call the resulting statistic a sample mean.

a. Arithmetic Mean
b. Unsolved problems in statistics
c. Interval estimation
d. Analysis of variance

27. In descriptive statistics, a _____ is any of the three values which divide the sorted data set into four equal parts, so that each part represents one fourth of the sampled population.

- first _____ = lower _____ = cuts off lowest 25% of data = 25th percentile
- second _____ = median = cuts data set in half = 50th percentile
- third _____ = upper _____ = cuts off highest 25% of data, or lowest 75% = 75th percentile

The difference between the upper and lower _____s is called the interquartile range.

There is no universal agreement on choosing the _____ values.

Chapter 10. STATISTICS

The formula for the position of the observation at a given percentile, y, with n data points sorted in ascending order is:

$$L_y = (n+1)(\frac{y}{100})$$

Example 4.
- a. Seven-number summary
- b. Quartile
- c. Trimean
- d. Mean reciprocal rank

28. A _____ is a device for performing mathematical calculations, distinguished from a computer by having a limited problem solving ability and an interface optimized for interactive calculation rather than programming. _____s can be hardware or software, and mechanical or electronic, and are often built into devices such as PDAs or mobile phones.

Modern electronic _____s are generally small, digital, and usually inexpensive.

- a. Calculator
- b. 1-center problem
- c. 2-3 heap
- d. 120-cell

29. In descriptive statistics, the _____ middle fifty and middle of the #s, is a measure of statistical dispersion, being equal to the difference between the third and first quartiles.

Unlike the range, the _____ is a robust statistic, having a breakdown point of 25%, and is thus often preferred to the total range.

The IQR is used to build box plots, simple graphical representations of a probability distribution.

- a. A Mathematical Theory of Communication
- b. Unitized risk
- c. A chemical equation
- d. Interquartile range

30. In descriptive statistics, the _____ is the length of the smallest interval which contains all the data. It is calculated by subtracting the smallest observations from the greatest and provides an indication of statistical dispersion.

It is measured in the same units as the data.

- a. Bandwidth
- b. Class
- c. Kernel
- d. Range

31. In mathematics and statistics, _____ is a measure of difference for interval and ratio variables between the observed value and the mean. The sign of _____, either positive or negative, indicates whether the observation is larger than or smaller than the mean. The magnitude of the value reports how different an observation is from the mean.
- a. Deviation
- b. Conchoid
- c. Functional
- d. Filter

32. In optics, _____ is the phenomenon in which the phase velocity of a wave depends on its frequency. Media having such a property are termed dispersive media.

The most familiar example of _____ is probably a rainbow, in which _____ causes the spatial separation of a white light into components of different wavelengths.

a. Crib
b. Depth
c. Boussinesq approximation
d. Dispersion

33. A _____ is the value of a variable below which a certain percent of observations fall. So the 20th _____ is the value below which 20 percent of the observations may be found. The term _____ and the related term _____ rank are often used in descriptive statistics as well as in the reporting of scores from norm-referenced tests.

a. Statistically significant
b. Percentile
c. Frequency distribution
d. Logistic regression

34. In probability and statistics, the _____ is a measure of the dispersion of a collection of numbers. It can apply to a probability distribution, a random variable, a population or a data set. The _____ is usually denoted with the letter σ.

a. Standard deviation
b. Statistical population
c. Null hypothesis
d. Failure rate

35. In probability theory and statistics, the _____ of a random variable, probability distribution averaging the squared distance of its possible values from the expected value. Whereas the mean is a way to describe the location of a distribution, the _____ is a way to capture its scale or degree of being spread out. The unit of _____ is the square of the unit of the original variable.

a. Variance
b. Probability distribution
c. Nonlinear regression
d. Kendall tau rank correlation coefficient

36. In a positional numeral system, the decimal separator is a symbol used to mark the boundary between the integral and the fractional parts of a decimal numeral. When used in context of Arabic numerals, terms implying the symbol used are _____ and decimal comma.

The decimal separator is mathematically a radix point.

a. Fibonacci coding
b. Hexadecimal
c. Tetradecimal
d. Decimal point

37. In mathematics, _____ and undefined are used to explain whether or not expressions have meaningful, sensible, and unambiguous values. Not all branches of mathematics come to the same conclusion.

The following expressions are undefined in all contexts, but remarks in the analysis section may apply.

a. Defined
b. LHS
c. Toy model
d. Plugging in

38. _____ is a dimensionless quantity derived by subtracting the population mean from an individual raw score and then dividing the difference by the population standard deviation.

Chapter 10. STATISTICS

a. 2-3 heap
b. 1-center problem
c. Z-score
d. 120-cell

39. In mathematics, the concept of a _____ tries to capture the intuitive idea of a geometrical one-dimensional and continuous object. A simple example is the circle. In everyday use of the term '_____', a straight line is not curved, but in mathematical parlance _____s include straight lines and line segments.
   a. Quadrifolium
   b. Curve
   c. Kappa curve
   d. Negative pedal curve

40. In differential geometry, a discipline within mathematics, a _____ is a subset of the tangent bundle of a manifold satisfying certain properties. _____s are used to build up notions of integrability, and specifically of a foliation of a manifold
   a. Constraint
   b. Discontinuity
   c. Coherence
   d. Distribution

41. The _____ or Dirac's delta is a mathematical construct introduced by the British theoretical physicist Paul Dirac. Informally, it is a function representing an infinitely sharp peak bounding unit area: a function that has the value zero everywhere except at x = 0 where its value is infinitely large in such a way that its total integral is 1. It is a continuous analogue of the discrete Kronecker delta.
   a. Dirac delta
   b. Hyperfunction
   c. Weak derivative
   d. Schwartz kernel theorem

42. In mathematics, specifically in combinatorial commutative algebra, a convex lattice polytope P is called _____ if it has the following property: given any positive integer n, every lattice point of the dilation nP, obtained from P by scaling its vertices by the factor n and taking the convex hull of the resulting points, can be written as the sum of exactly n lattice points in P. This property plays an important role in the theory of toric varieties, where it corresponds to projective normality of the toric variety determined by P.

The simplex in R^k with the vertices at the origin and along the unit coordinate vectors is _____.

   a. Normal
   b. Polytetrahedron
   c. Hypercube
   d. Demihypercubes

43. A _____ is a circular chart divided into sectors, illustrating relative magnitudes or frequences or percents. In a _____, the arc length of each sector, is proportional to the quantity it represents. Together, the sectors create a full disk.
   a. 2-3 heap
   b. 120-cell
   c. 1-center problem
   d. Pie chart

44. In statistics, a _____ is a list of the values that a variable takes in a sample. It is usually a list, ordered by quantity, showing the number of times each value appears. For example, if 100 people rate a five-point Likert scale assessing their agreement with a statement on a scale on which 1 denotes strong agreement and 5 strong disagreement, the _____ of their responses might look like:

This simple tabulation has two drawbacks.

a. Percentile
c. Frequency Distribution
b. Confounding
d. Covariance

45. The _____ is an important family of continuous probability distributions, applicable in many fields. Each member of the family may be defined by two parameters, location and scale: the mean and variance respectively. The standard _____ is the _____ with a mean of zero and a variance of one.
- a. Percentile rank
- b. Coefficient of variation
- c. Null hypothesis
- d. Normal distribution

46. The framework of quantum mechanics requires a careful definition of _____, and a thorough discussion of its practical and philosophical implications.

_____ is viewed in different ways in the many interpretations of quantum mechanics; however, despite the considerable philosophical differences, they almost universally agree on the practical question of what results from a routine quantum-physics laboratory _____. To describe this, a simple framework to use is the Copenhagen interpretation, and it will be implicitly used in this section; the utility of this approach has been verified countless times, and all other interpretations are necessarily constructed so as to give the same quantitative predictions as this in almost every case.

- a. 1-center problem
- b. Fundamental units
- c. Dynamic range
- d. Measurement

47. In statistics, a _____ is a subset of a population. Typically, the population is very large, making a census or a complete enumeration of all the values in the population impractical or impossible. The _____ represents a subset of manageable size.
- a. Sample
- b. Boussinesq approximation
- c. Duality
- d. Dispersion

Chapter 11. PROBABILITY

1. _____ is the likelihood or chance that something is the case or will happen. Theoretical _____ is used extensively in areas such as statistics, mathematics, science and philosophy to draw conclusions about the likelihood of potential events and the underlying mechanics of complex systems.

The word _____ does not have a consistent direct definition.

a. Statistical significance
b. Discrete random variable
c. Standardized moment
d. Probability

2. In game theory, a player's _____ in a game is a complete plan of action for whatever situation might arise; this fully determines the player's behaviour. A player's _____ will determine the action the player will take at any stage of the game, for every possible history of play up to that stage.

A _____ profile is a set of strategies for each player which fully specifies all actions in a game.

a. Strategy
b. Matching pennies
c. Sir Philip Sidney game
d. Correlated equilibrium

3. In scientific inquiry, an _____ is a method of investigating particular types of research questions or solving particular types of problems. The _____ is a cornerstone in the empirical approach to acquiring deeper knowledge about the world and is used in both natural sciences as well as in social sciences. An _____ is defined, in science, as a method of investigating less known fields, solving practical problems and proving theoretical assumptions.

a. A Mathematical Theory of Communication
b. A chemical equation
c. A posteriori
d. Experiment

4. In abstract algebra, a module S over a ring R is called _____ or irreducible if it is not the zero module 0 and if its only submodules are 0 and S. Understanding the _____ modules over a ring is usually helpful because these modules form the 'building blocks' of all other modules in a certain sense.

Abelian groups are the same as Z-modules.

a. Harmonic series
b. Derivation
c. Basis
d. Simple

5. In probability theory, an _____ is a set of outcomes to which a probability is assigned. Typically, when the sample space is finite, any subset of the sample space is an _____. However, this approach does not work well in cases where the sample space is infinite, most notably when the outcome is a real number.

a. Equaliser
b. Audio compression
c. Information set
d. Event

6. In game theory, an _____ is a set of moves or strategies taken by the players, or their payoffs resulting from the actions or strategies taken by all players. The two are complementary in that given knowledge of the set of strategies of all players, the final state of the game is known, as are any relevant payoffs. In a game where chance or a random event is involved, the _____ is not known from only the set of strategies, but is only realized when the random even are realized.

a. Algebraic
b. Equaliser
c. Autonomous system
d. Outcome

7. In statistics, a _____ is a subset of a population. Typically, the population is very large, making a census or a complete enumeration of all the values in the population impractical or impossible. The _____ represents a subset of manageable size.
 a. Boussinesq approximation
 b. Duality
 c. Dispersion
 d. Sample

8. In probability theory, the _____ or universal _____, often denoted S, Ω of an experiment or random trial is the set of all possible outcomes. For example, if the experiment is tossing a coin, the _____ is the set {head, tail}. For tossing a single six-sided die, the _____ is {1, 2, 3, 4, 5, 6}.
 a. Marginal distribution
 b. Markov chain
 c. Sample space
 d. Martingale central limit theorem

9. _____ is usually defined as the activity of using and developing computer technology, computer hardware and software. It is the computer-specific part of information technology. Computer science (or _____ science) is the study and the science of the theoretical foundations of information and computation and their implementation and application in computer systems.
 a. Probabilistic Turing Machine
 b. Deterministic finite state machine
 c. Parallel Random Access Machine
 d. Computing

10. In probability theory and statistics the _____ in favour of an event or a proposition are the quantity p /, where p is the probability of the event or proposition. The _____ against the same event are / p. For example, if you chose a random day of the week, then the _____ that you would choose a Sunday would be 1/6, not 1/7.
 a. Event
 b. Anscombe transform
 c. Odds
 d. Estimation of covariance matrices

11. In the mathematics of probability, an _____ is an event x with a probability Pr of zero, or Pr(x) = 0.

An _____ is not the same as the stronger concept of logical impossibility. For any continuous probability distribution the probability of any single elementary event is 0, yet the event is not logically impossible as an event outside the distribution.

 a. A Mathematical Theory of Communication
 b. A posteriori
 c. Impossible event
 d. A chemical equation

12. _____ are small polyhedral objects, usually cubic, used for generating random numbers or other symbols. This makes _____ suitable as gambling devices, especially for craps or sic bo, or for use in non-gambling tabletop games.

A traditional die is a cube, marked on each of its six faces with a different number of circular patches or pits called pips.

 a. Dice
 b. 1-center problem
 c. 2-3 heap
 d. 120-cell

Chapter 11. PROBABILITY

13. In discrete mathematics and predominantly in set theory, a _____ is a concept used in comparisons of sets to refer to the unique values of one set in relation to another. The terms 'absolute' and 'relative' _____ refer to more specific applications of the concept, with universal _____s referring to elements unique to the universal set and the latter referring to the unique elements of one set in relation to another. In this image, the universal set is represented by the border of the image, and the set A as a disc.

a. Kernel
b. Huge
c. Derivative algebra
d. Complement

14. A _____ is a 2D geometric symbolic representation of information according to some visualization technique. Sometimes, the technique uses a 3D visualization which is then projected onto the 2D surface. The word graph is sometimes used as a synonym for _____.

a. 1-center problem
b. 120-cell
c. 2-3 heap
d. Diagram

15. In simple terms, two events are _____ if they cannot occur at the same time.

In logic, two _____ propositions are propositions that logically cannot both be true. To say that more than two propositions are _____ may, depending on context mean that no two of them can both be true, or only that they cannot all be true.

a. Philosophy
b. Philosophy of mathematics
c. Determinism
d. Mutually exclusive

16. In set theory, a _____ is a partially ordered set such that for each t ∈ T, the set {s ∈ T : s < t} is well-ordered by the relation <. For each t ∈ T, the order type of {s ∈ T : s < t} is called the height of t. The height of T itself is the least ordinal greater than the height of each element of T.

a. Definable numbers
b. Set-theoretic topology
c. Transitive reduction
d. Tree

17. _____ is the mathematical operation of scaling one number by another. It is one of the four basic operations in elementary arithmetic.

_____ is defined for whole numbers in terms of repeated addition; for example, 4 multiplied by 3 can be calculated by adding 3 copies of 4 together:

$$4 + 4 + 4 = 12.$$

_____ of rational numbers and real numbers is defined by systematic generalization of this basic idea.

a. The number 0 is even.
b. Highest common factor
c. Least common multiple
d. Multiplication

18. A _____ is one of the basic shapes of geometry: a polygon with three corners or vertices and three sides or edges which are line segments. A _____ with vertices A, B, and C is denoted ABC.

In Euclidean geometry any three non-collinear points determine a unique _____ and a unique plane.

a. Kepler triangle
c. 1-center problem
b. Fuhrmann circle
d. Triangle

19. A _____, from the French patron, is a type of theme of recurring events of or objects, sometimes referred to as elements of a set. These elements repeat in a predictable manner. It can be a template or model which can be used to generate things or parts of a thing, especially if the things that are created have enough in common for the underlying _____ to be inferred, in which case the things are said to exhibit the unique _____.

a. 2-3 heap
c. 1-center problem
b. Pattern
d. 120-cell

20. A _____ is a computational or physical device designed to generate a sequence of numbers or symbols that lack any pattern. Computer-based systems for random number generation are widely used, but often fall short of this goal, though they may meet some statistical tests for randomness intended to ensure that they do not have any easily discernible patterns. Methods for generating random results have existed since ancient times, including dice, coin flipping, the shuffling of playing cards, the use of yarrow stalks in the I Ching, and many other techniques.

a. Shannon limit
c. Constant-weight code
b. Random number generator
d. Typical set

21. In probability theory and statistics, the _____ of a random variable is the integral of the random variable with respect to its probability measure. For discrete random variables this is equivalent to the probability-weighted sum of the possible values, and for continuous random variables with a density function it is the probability density -weighted integral of the possible values.

The _____ may be intuitively understood by the law of large numbers: The _____, when it exists, is almost surely the limit of the sample mean as sample size grows to infinity.

a. Illustration
c. Event
b. Expected value
d. Infinitely divisible distribution

22. _____ is the probability of some event A, given the occurrence of some other event B. _____ is written P[A | B], and is read 'the probability of A, given B'.

Joint probability is the probability of two events in conjunction. That is, it is the probability of both events together. The joint probability of A and B is written $P(A \cap B)$ or $P(A, B)$.

a. Conditional Probability
c. Quantile
b. Renewal theory
d. Sample space

23. _____ or set diagrams are diagrams that show all hypothetically possible logical relations between a finite collection of sets. _____ were invented around 1880 by John Venn. They are used in many fields, including set theory, probability, logic, statistics, and computer science.

a. 1-center problem
c. 120-cell
b. Venn diagrams
d. 2-3 heap

24. In several fields of mathematics the term _____ is used with different but closely related meanings. They all relate to the notion of mapping the elements of a set to other elements of the same set, i.e., exchanging elements of a set.

Chapter 11. PROBABILITY

The general concept of _____ can be defined more formally in different contexts:

In combinatorics, a _____ is usually understood to be a sequence containing each element from a finite set once, and only once.

a. Tensor product
b. Linearly independent
c. Cyclic permutation
d. Permutation

25. In combinatorial mathematics, a _____ is an un-ordered collection of distinct elements, usually of a prescribed size and taken from a given set. Given such a set S, a _____ of elements of S is just a subset of S, where as always forsets the order of the elements is not taken into account. Also, as always forsets, no elements can be repeated more than once in a _____; this is often referred to as a 'collection without repetition'.

a. Fill-in
b. Sparsity
c. Heawood number
d. Combination

26. In mathematics, the _____ of a non-negative integer n, denoted by n!, is the product of all positive integers less than or equal to n. For example,

$$5! = 1 \times 2 \times 3 \times 4 \times 5 = 120$$

and
$$6! = 1 \times 2 \times 3 \times 4 \times 5 \times 6 = 720$$

The notation n! was introduced by Christian Kramp in 1808.

The _____ function is formally defined by

$$n! = \prod_{k=1}^{n} k \qquad \forall n \in \mathbb{N}.$$

The above definition incorporates the instance

$$0! = 1$$

as an instance of the fact that the product of no numbers at all is 1.

a. Factorial
b. Plane partition
c. Partition of a set
d. Symbolic combinatorics

27. In cryptography, _____ is a pseudorandom number generator and a stream cipher designed by Robert Jenkins to be cryptographically secure. The name is an acronym for Indirection, Shift, Accumulate, Add, and Count.

The _____ algorithm has similarities with RC4.

a. Imputation
c. Order
b. Introduction
d. Isaac

28. The _____ (symbol: N) is the SI derived unit of force, named after Isaac _____ in recognition of his work on classical mechanics.

The _____ is the unit of force derived in the SI system; it is equal to the amount of force required to accelerate a mass of one kilogram at a rate of one meter per second per second. Algebraically:

$$1\ N = 1\ \frac{kg \cdot m}{s^2}.$$

- 1 N is the force of Earth's gravity on an object with a mass of about 102 g ($\frac{1}{9.8}$ kg) (such as a small apple.)
- On Earth's surface, a mass of 1 kg exerts a force of approximately 9.80665 N [down] (or 1 kgf.) The approximation of 1 kg corresponding to 10 N is sometimes used as a rule of thumb in everyday life and in engineering.
- The force of Earth's gravity on a human being with a mass of 70 kg is approximately 687 N.
- The dot product of force and distance is mechanical work. Thus, in SI units, a force of 1 N exerted over a distance of 1 m is 1 N·m of work. The Work-Energy Theorem states that the work done on a body is equal to the change in energy of the body. 1 N·m = 1 J (joule), the SI unit of energy.
- It is common to see forces expressed in kilonewtons or kN, where 1 kN = 1 000 N.

a. Newton
c. 1-center problem
b. 2-3 heap
d. 120-cell

29. In classical differential geometry, _____ refers to the simple idea of rolling one smooth surface over another in Euclidean space. For example, the tangent plane to a surface at a point can be rolled around the surface to obtain the tangent-plane at other points.

The tangential contact between the surfaces being rolled over one another provides a relation between points on the two surfaces.

a. Development
c. Blinding
b. Double counting
d. FISH

30. _____ is a part of mathematics concerned with questions of size, shape, and relative position of figures and with properties of space. _____ is one of the oldest sciences. Initially a body of practical knowledge concerning lengths, areas, and volumes, in the third century BC _____ was put into an axiomatic form by Euclid, whose treatment--Euclidean _____--set a standard for many centuries to follow.

a. 120-cell
b. 1-center problem
c. 2-3 heap
d. Geometry

31. The word _____ has many distinct meanings in different fields of knowledge, depending on their methodologies and the context of discussion. Broadly speaking we can say that a _____ is some kind of belief or claim that (supposedly) explains, asserts, or consolidates some class of claims. Additionally, in contrast with a theorem the statement of the _____ is generally accepted only in some tentative fashion as opposed to regarding it as having been conclusively established.

a. Per mil
b. Transport of structure
c. Defined
d. Theory

32. StanisÅ‚aw Marcin Ulam (April 13, 1909 - May 13, 1984) was a Polish mathematician who participated in the Manhattan Project and proposed the Teller-Ulam design of thermonuclear weapons. He also invented nuclear pulse propulsion and developed a number of mathematical tools in number theory, set theory, ergodic theory, and algebraic topology.

_____ was born to a Polish Jewish family in Lwów , Galicia, then in Austria-Hungary; since 1918 in Poland and since 1939 in USSR.

a. Agnes Meyer Driscoll
b. Abraham Sinkov
c. Stanislaw Ulam
d. Adi Shamir

Chapter 12. GEOMETRIC SHAPES

1.

_____ is a Unicode block of 96 symbols at hex codepoint range 25A0-25FF. This range contains various _____.

Only two font sets--Code2000 and the DejaVu family--include coverage for each of the glyphs in the _____ range.

- a. 120-cell
- b. 2-3 heap
- c. 1-center problem
- d. Geometric shapes

2. The _____ of an object located in some space refers to the part of space occupied by the object as determined by its external boundary -- abstracting from other aspects the object may have such as its colour, content as well as from the object's position and orientation in space, and its size.

According to famous mathematician and statistician David George Kendall, _____ may be defined as

Simple two-dimensional _____s can be described by basic geometry such as points, line, curves, plane, and so on. _____s that occur in the physical world are often quite complex; they may be arbitrarily curved as studied by differential geometry as for plants or coastlines.)

- a. Confocal
- b. Spidron
- c. Parallel lines
- d. Shape

3. In game theory, a player's _____ in a game is a complete plan of action for whatever situation might arise; this fully determines the player's behaviour. A player's _____ will determine the action the player will take at any stage of the game, for every possible history of play up to that stage.

A _____ profile is a set of strategies for each player which fully specifies all actions in a game.

- a. Correlated equilibrium
- b. Strategy
- c. Matching pennies
- d. Sir Philip Sidney game

4. In classical differential geometry, _____ refers to the simple idea of rolling one smooth surface over another in Euclidean space. For example, the tangent plane to a surface at a point can be rolled around the surface to obtain the tangent-plane at other points.

The tangential contact between the surfaces being rolled over one another provides a relation between points on the two surfaces.

- a. Blinding
- b. FISH
- c. Double counting
- d. Development

Chapter 12. GEOMETRIC SHAPES

5. _____ is a part of mathematics concerned with questions of size, shape, and relative position of figures and with properties of space. _____ is one of the oldest sciences. Initially a body of practical knowledge concerning lengths, areas, and volumes, in the third century BC _____ was put into an axiomatic form by Euclid, whose treatment--Euclidean _____--set a standard for many centuries to follow.
   a. 1-center problem
   b. 120-cell
   c. 2-3 heap
   d. Geometry

6. The word _____ has many distinct meanings in different fields of knowledge, depending on their methodologies and the context of discussion. Broadly speaking we can say that a _____ is some kind of belief or claim that (supposedly) explains, asserts, or consolidates some class of claims. Additionally, in contrast with a theorem the statement of the _____ is generally accepted only in some tentative fashion as opposed to regarding it as having been conclusively established.
   a. Defined
   b. Transport of structure
   c. Per mil
   d. Theory

7. _____ is a dissection puzzle consisting of 7 flat shapes called tans, which fit together to form a shape of some sort. The objective is to form a specific shape with seven pieces. The shape has to contain all the pieces, which must not overlap and touch each other.
   a. Tantrix
   b. Mutilated chessboard
   c. 1-center problem
   d. Tangram

8. A _____ undone, which forms a cube _____ cube; a type of _____

A _____ is a problem or enigma that challenges ingenuity. In a basic _____ one is intended to piece together objects (_____ pieces) in a logical way in order to come up with the desired shape, picture or solution. _____s are often contrived as a form of entertainment, but they can also stem from serious mathematical or logistical problems -- in such cases, their successful resolution can be a significant contribution to mathematical research .

   a. The Doctrine of Chances
   b. Visible
   c. The Code Book
   d. Puzzle

9. In geometry, a _____ is a polygon with four sides or edges and four vertices or corners. Sometimes, the term quadrangle is used, for etymological symmetry with triangle, and sometimes tetragon for consistency with pentagon, hexagon and so on. The interior angles of a _____ add up to 360 degrees of arc.
   a. 120-cell
   b. Quadrilateral
   c. 1-center problem
   d. 2-3 heap

10. In geometry and trigonometry, an _____ is the figure formed by two rays sharing a common endpoint, called the vertex of the _____. The magnitude of the _____ is the 'amount of rotation' that separates the two rays, and can be measured by considering the length of circular arc swept out when one ray is rotated about the vertex to coincide with the other. Where there is no possibility of confusion, the term '_____' is used interchangeably for both the geometric configuration itself and for its angular magnitude.
   a. A posteriori
   b. A chemical equation
   c. A Mathematical Theory of Communication
   d. Angle

Chapter 12. GEOMETRIC SHAPES

11. In geometry, an _____ is a triangle in which all three sides have equal lengths. In traditional or Euclidean geometry, _____s are also equiangular; that is, all three internal angles are also equal to each other and are each 60°. They are regular polygons, and can therefore also be referred to as regular triangles.
   a. A chemical equation
   b. Equilateral triangle
   c. A Mathematical Theory of Communication
   d. Isotomic conjugate

12. A _____ is a flying tethered object that depends upon the tension of a tethering system. The necessary lift that makes the _____ wing fly is generated when air flows over and under the _____'s wing, producing low pressure above the wing and high pressure below it. This deflection also generates horizontal drag along the direction of the wind.
   a. 2-3 heap
   b. Kite
   c. 1-center problem
   d. 120-cell

13. In mathematics, especially in geometry and group theory, a _____ in R^n is a discrete subgroup of R^n which spans the real vector space R^n. Every _____ in R^n can be generated from a basis for the vector space by forming all linear combinations with integral coefficients. A _____ may be viewed as a regular tiling of a space by a primitive cell.
   a. Homogeneity
   b. Group
   c. Lattice
   d. Boundary

14. In geometry, a _____ is a part of a line that is bounded by two distinct end points, and contains every point on the line between its end points. Examples of _____s include the sides of a triangle or square. More generally, when the end points are both vertices of a polygon, the _____ is either an edge if they are adjacent vertices, or otherwise a diagonal.
   a. Golden angle
   b. Line segment
   c. Cuboid
   d. Transversal line

15. In geometry, a _____ is a quadrilateral with two sets of parallel sides. The opposite sides of a _____ are of equal length, and the opposite angles of a _____ are congruent. The three-dimensional counterpart of a _____ is a parallelepiped.
   a. 2-3 heap
   b. 1-center problem
   c. 120-cell
   d. Parallelogram

16. In geometry, a _____ is defined as a quadrilateral where all four of its angles are right angles.
   a. Rectangle
   b. Cantor-Dedekind axiom
   c. Point group in two dimensions
   d. Polytope

17. In mathematics, the _____ is one of the five two-dimensional lattice types. It is the two-dimensional version of the integer lattice.

Two orientations of an image of the lattice are by far the most common.

   a. Homothetic center
   b. Square lattice
   c. Half-space
   d. Rotation

18. A _____ is one of the basic shapes of geometry: a polygon with three corners or vertices and three sides or edges which are line segments. A _____ with vertices A, B, and C is denoted ABC.

In Euclidean geometry any three non-collinear points determine a unique _____ and a unique plane.

Chapter 12. GEOMETRIC SHAPES

a. Fuhrmann circle
b. 1-center problem
c. Kepler triangle
d. Triangle

19. In geometry, a _____ is a special kind of point, usually a corner of a polygon, polyhedron, or higher dimensional polytope. In the geometry of curves a _____ is a point of where the first derivative of curvature is zero. In graph theory, a _____ is the fundamental unit out of which graphs are formed
    a. Vertex
    b. Dini
    c. Duality
    d. Crib

20. In geometry, two sets of points are called _____ if one can be transformed into the other by an isometry. Less formally, two figures are _____ if they have the same shape and size, but are in different positions.

In a Euclidean system, congruence is fundamental; it is the counterpart of equality for numbers.

   a. Congruent
   b. Germ
   c. Gamma test
   d. Function

21. In geometry and trigonometry, a _____ is defined as an angle between two straight intersecting lines of ninety degrees, or one-quarter of a circle.
    a. Trigonometric functions
    b. Sine integral
    c. Trigonometry
    d. Right angle

22. An _____ is a quadrilateral with a line of symmetry bisecting one pair of opposite sides, making it automatically a trapezoid. Two opposite sides are parallel, the two other sides are of equal length. The diagonals are of equal length.
    a. A chemical equation
    b. A posteriori
    c. A Mathematical Theory of Communication
    d. Isosceles trapezoid

23. In geometry a _____ is traditionally a plane figure that is bounded by a closed path or circuit, composed of a finite sequence of straight line segments. These segments are called its edges or sides, and the points where two edges meet are the _____'s vertices or corners. The interior of the _____ is sometimes called its body.
    a. Polygonal curve
    b. Parallelogon
    c. Polygon
    d. Regular polygon

24. In geometry, a _____ , or rhomb is an equilateral parallelogram. In other words, it is a four-sided polygon in which every side has the same length.

The _____ is often casually called a diamond, after the diamonds suit in playing cards, or a lozenge, because those shapes are rhombi, although rhombi are not necessarily diamonds or lozenges.

   a. 120-cell
   b. Rhombus
   c. 2-3 heap
   d. 1-center problem

25. A _____ or a trapezium is a quadrilateral that has at least one pair of parallel lines for sides.

Some authors define it as a quadrilateral having exactly one pair of parallel sides, so as to exclude parallelograms, which otherwise would be regarded as a special type of _____, but most mathematicians use the inclusive definition.

In North America, the term trapezium is used to refer to a quadrilateral with no parallel sides.

a. Trapezium
b. Lozenge
c. Rhomboid
d. Trapezoid

26. In mathematics and computer science, _____ (also base-16, hexa or base, of 16. It uses sixteen distinct symbols, most often the symbols 0-9 to represent values zero to nine, and A, B, C, D, E, F (or a through f) to represent values ten to fifteen.

Its primary use is as a human friendly representation of binary coded values, so it is often used in digital electronics and computer engineering.

a. Hexadecimal
b. Factoradic
c. Tetradecimal
d. Radix

27. In Euclidean geometry, an _____ is a polygon whose vertex angles are equal. If the lengths of the sides are also equal then it is a regular polygon.

The only equiangular triangle is the equilateral triangle.

a. Axial symmetry
b. Uniform coloring
c. Analytic space
d. Equiangular Polygon

28. In geometry, an _____ is a polygon which has all sides of the same length.

For instance, an equilateral triangle is a triangle of equal edge lengths. All equilateral triangles are similar to each other, and have 60 degree internal angles.

a. A Mathematical Theory of Communication
b. Enneagon
c. Octagon
d. Equilateral Polygon

29. _____, line symmetry, mirror symmetry, mirror-image symmetry, or bilateral symmetry is symmetry with respect to reflection.

In 2D there is an axis of symmetry, in 3D a plane of symmetry. An object or figure which is indistinguishable from its transformed image is called mirror symmetric (see mirror image.)

a. Circumscribed sphere
b. Reflection symmetry
c. Hypotenuse
d. Line segment

Chapter 12. GEOMETRIC SHAPES

30. _____ generally conveys two primary meanings. The first is an imprecise sense of harmonious or aesthetically-pleasing proportionality and balance; such that it reflects beauty or perfection. The second meaning is a precise and well-defined concept of balance or 'patterned self-similarity' that can be demonstrated or proved according to the rules of a formal system: by geometry, through physics or otherwise.
   a. Tessellation
   b. Molecular symmetry
   c. Symmetry breaking
   d. Symmetry

31. A _____ is a movement of an object in a circular motion. A two-dimensional object rotates around a center of _____. A three-dimensional object rotates around a line called an axis.
   a. Rotation
   b. Steiner-Lehmus theorem
   c. Square lattice
   d. Homothetic center

32. Generally speaking, an object with _____ is an object that looks the same after a certain amount of rotation. An object may have more than one _____; for instance, if reflections or turning it over are not counted, the triskelion appearing on the Isle of Man's flag has three rotational symmetries. More examples may be seen below.
   a. 120-cell
   b. 1-center problem
   c. 2-3 heap
   d. Rotational symmetry

33. A _____ of a curve is the envelope of a family of congruent circles centered on the curve. It generalises the concept of _____ lines.

It is sometimes called the offset curve but the term 'offset' often refers also to translation.

   a. Cycloid
   b. Cissoid
   c. Parallel
   d. Bifolium

34. The existence and properties of _____ are the basis of Euclid's parallel postulate. _____ are two lines on the same plane that do not intersect even assuming that lines extend to infinity in either direction.
   a. Vertical translation
   b. Spidron
   c. Square wheel
   d. Parallel lines

35. In mathematics, the _____ is an approach to finding a particular solution to certain inhomogeneous ordinary differential equations and recurrence relations. It is closely related to the annihilator method, but instead of using a particular kind of differential operator in order to find the best possible form of the particular solution, a 'guess' is made as to the appropriate form, which is then tested by differentiating the resulting equation. In this sense, the _____ is less formal but more intuitive than the annihilator method.
   a. Phase line
   b. Linear differential equation
   c. Method of undetermined coefficients
   d. Differential algebraic equations

36. In mathematics, the concept of a _____ tries to capture the intuitive idea of a geometrical one-dimensional and continuous object. A simple example is the circle. In everyday use of the term '_____', a straight line is not curved, but in mathematical parlance _____s include straight lines and line segments.
   a. Curve
   b. Kappa curve
   c. Negative pedal curve
   d. Quadrifolium

Chapter 12. GEOMETRIC SHAPES

37. In cryptography, _____ is a pseudorandom number generator and a stream cipher designed by Robert Jenkins to be cryptographically secure. The name is an acronym for Indirection, Shift, Accumulate, Add, and Count.

The _____ algorithm has similarities with RC4.

a. Introduction
c. Imputation
b. Isaac
d. Order

38. The _____ (symbol: N) is the SI derived unit of force, named after Isaac _____ in recognition of his work on classical mechanics.

The _____ is the unit of force derived in the SI system; it is equal to the amount of force required to accelerate a mass of one kilogram at a rate of one meter per second per second. Algebraically:

$$1 \text{ N} = 1 \; \frac{\text{kg} \cdot \text{m}}{\text{s}^2}.$$

- 1 N is the force of Earth's gravity on an object with a mass of about 102 g ($1/_{9.8}$ kg) (such as a small apple.)
- On Earth's surface, a mass of 1 kg exerts a force of approximately 9.80665 N [down] (or 1 kgf.) The approximation of 1 kg corresponding to 10 N is sometimes used as a rule of thumb in everyday life and in engineering.
- The force of Earth's gravity on a human being with a mass of 70 kg is approximately 687 N.
- The dot product of force and distance is mechanical work. Thus, in SI units, a force of 1 N exerted over a distance of 1 m is 1 N·m of work. The Work-Energy Theorem states that the work done on a body is equal to the change in energy of the body. 1 N·m = 1 J (joule), the SI unit of energy.
- It is common to see forces expressed in kilonewtons or kN, where 1 kN = 1 000 N.

a. 1-center problem
c. 120-cell
b. 2-3 heap
d. Newton

39. In geometry, an _____ is a polygon that has eight sides. A regular _____ is represented by the Schläfli symbol {8}. A regular _____ is constructible with compass and straightedge.

a. Equilateral polygon
c. Enneagon
b. Octagon
d. A Mathematical Theory of Communication

40. In abstract algebra, a module S over a ring R is called _____ or irreducible if it is not the zero module 0 and if its only submodules are 0 and S. Understanding the _____ modules over a ring is usually helpful because these modules form the 'building blocks' of all other modules in a certain sense.

Abelian groups are the same as Z-modules.

Chapter 12. GEOMETRIC SHAPES

a. Basis
b. Harmonic series
c. Derivation
d. Simple

41. In mathematics, specifically in combinatorial commutative algebra, a convex lattice polytope P is called _____ if it has the following property: given any positive integer n, every lattice point of the dilation nP, obtained from P by scaling its vertices by the factor n and taking the convex hull of the resulting points, can be written as the sum of exactly n lattice points in P. This property plays an important role in the theory of toric varieties, where it corresponds to projective normality of the toric variety determined by P.

The simplex in R^k with the vertices at the origin and along the unit coordinate vectors is _____.

a. Hypercube
b. Normal
c. Polytetrahedron
d. Demihypercubes

42. _____ are used in computer graphics to compose images that are three-dimensional in appearance. Usually triangular, _____ arise when an object's surface is modeled, vertices are selected, and the object is rendered in a wire frame model. This is quicker to display than a shaded model; thus the _____ are a stage in computer animation.

a. Triskaidecagon
b. Polygons
c. Visibility polygon
d. Heptadecagon

43. A _____ is a polygon which is equiangular and equilateral. _____s may be convex or star.

These properties apply to both convex and star _____s.

a. Regular decagon
b. Constructible polygon
c. Star-shaped polygon
d. Regular Polygon

44. The term _____ or centre is used in various contexts in abstract algebra to denote the set of all those elements that commute with all other elements. More specifically:

- The _____ of a group G consists of all those elements x in G such that xg = gx for all g in G. This is a normal subgroup of G.
- The _____ of a ring R is the subset of R consisting of all those elements x of R such that xr = rx for all r in R. The _____ is a commutative subring of R, so R is an algebra over its _____.
- The _____ of an algebra A consists of all those elements x of A such that xa = ax for all a in A. See also: central simple algebra.
- The _____ of a Lie algebra L consists of all those elements x in L such that [x,a] = 0 for all a in L. This is an ideal of the Lie algebra L.
- The _____ of a monoidal category C consists of pairs *a natural isomorphism satisfying certain axioms*.

a. Block size
b. Center
c. Brute Force
d. Disk

Chapter 12. GEOMETRIC SHAPES

45. A _____ is an angle whose Line is the center of a circle, and whose sides pass through a pair of points on the circle, thereby subtending an arc between those two points whose angle is equal to the _____ itself. It is also known as the arc segment's angular distance.

On a sphere or ellipsoid, the _____ is delineated along a great circle.

  a. Mirror image
  b. Hypotenuse
  c. Line segment
  d. Central angle

46. A _____ is a simple shape of Euclidean geometry consisting of those points in a plane which are at a constant distance, called the radius, from a fixed point, called the center. A _____ with center A is sometimes denoted by the symbol A.

A chord of a _____ is a line segment whose two endpoints lie on the _____.

  a. Circumcircle
  b. Circular segment
  c. Malfatti circles
  d. Circle

47. In mathematics, a real-valued function f defined on an interval is called _____, concave upwards, concave up or _____ cup, if for any two points x and y in its domain C and any t in [0,1], we have

$$f(tx + (1-t)y) \leq tf(x) + (1-t)f(y).$$

_____ function on an interval.

In other words, a function is _____ if and only if its epigraph is a _____ set.

Pictorially, a function is called '_____' if the function lies below the straight line segment connecting two points, for any two points in the interval.

A function is called strictly _____ if

$$f(tx + (1-t)y) < tf(x) + (1-t)f(y)$$

for any t in and $x \neq y$.

A function f is said to be concave if − f is _____.

  a. Convex
  b. Continuum
  c. Continuous wavelet
  d. Contrapositive

48. In geometry, a polygon can be either convex or concave.

Chapter 12. GEOMETRIC SHAPES

A _____ is a simple polygon whose interior is a convex set. The following properties of a simple polygon are all equivalent to convexity:

- Every internal angle is less than 180 degrees or equal to 180 degrees.
- Every line segment between two vertices of the polygon does not go exterior to the polygon.

A simple polygon is strictly convex if every internal angle is strictly less than 180 degrees. Equivalently, a polygon is strictly convex if every line segment between two nonadjacent vertices of the polygon is strictly interior to the polygon except at its endpoints.

a. Claw-free permutations
b. Charles's Law
c. Continuous phase modulation
d. Convex polygon

49. In general topology and related areas of mathematics, the _____ (inductive topology or strong topology) on a set X, with respect to a family of functions into X, is the finest topology on X which makes those functions continuous.

Given a set X and a family of topological spaces Y_i with functions

$$f_i : Y_i \to X$$

the _____ τ on X is the finest topology such that each

$$f_i : Y_i \to (X, \tau)$$

is continuous.

Explicitly, the _____ may be described as follows: a subset U of X is open if and only if $f_i^{-1}(U)$ is open in Y_i for each i ∈ I.

a. Wallman compactification
b. Gluing axiom
c. Cylinder set
d. Final topology

50. An _____ is an angle formed by one side of a simple polygon and a line extended from that side.
a. Angular diameter
b. Exterior angle
c. Orthogon
d. Interior angle

51. In geometry, an _____ is an angle formed by two sides of a simple polygon that share an endpoint, namely, the angle on the inner side of the polygon. A simple polygon has exactly one internal angle per vertex.

If every internal angle of a polygon is at most 180 degrees, the polygon is called convex.

a. Angle bisector
b. Exterior angle
c. Interior angle
d. Angle chasing

52. In classical geometry, a _____ of a circle or sphere is any line segment from its center to its boundary. By extension, the _____ of a circle or sphere is the length of any such segment. The _____ is half the diameter. In science and engineering the term _____ of curvature is commonly used as a synonym for _____.
    a. Non-Euclidean geometry
    b. Duoprism
    c. Birational geometry
    d. Radius

53. In geometry, the _____, geometric center, or barycenter of a plane figure X is the intersection of all straight lines that divide X into two parts of equal moment about the line. Informally, it is the 'average' of all points of X. The definition extends to any object X in n-dimensional space: its _____ is the intersection of all hyperplanes that divide X into two parts of equal moment about the hyperplane.
    a. 1-center problem
    b. 120-cell
    c. Centroid
    d. Line element

54. In mathematics, a _____ is a natural number which has exactly two distinct natural number divisors: 1 and itself. An infinitude of _____s exists, as demonstrated by Euclid around 300 BC. The first twenty-five _____s are:

    2, 3, 5, 7, 11, 13, 17, 19, 23, 29, 31, 37, 41, 43, 47, 53, 59, 61, 67, 71, 73, 79, 83, 89, 97.

    a. Perrin number
    b. Pronic number
    c. Highly composite number
    d. Prime number

55. A _____, magnetic _____ or mariner's _____ is a navigational instrument for determining direction relative to the earth's magnetic poles. It consists of a magnetized pointer (usually marked on the North end) free to align itself with Earth's magnetic field. The face of the _____ generally highlights the cardinal points of north, south, east and west.
    a. 1-center problem
    b. Compass
    c. 120-cell
    d. Torquetum

56. As an abstract term, _____ means similarity between objects.
    a. Congruence
    b. 2-3 heap
    c. 120-cell
    d. 1-center problem

57. In geometry, three or more lines are said to be _____ if they intersect at a single point.

In a triangle, four basic types of _____ lines are altitudes, angle bisectors, medians, and perpendicular bisectors:

- In a triangle, altitudes run from each vertex and meet the opposite side at right-angles. The point where three altitudes meet is the orthocenter.

- Angle bisectors are rays running from the bisector of each angle of the triangle. They all meet at the incenter.

- Medians connect the vertexes in a triangle to the midpoint of the opposite side. They meet at the centroid.

Chapter 12. GEOMETRIC SHAPES

a. Dini
b. Kernel
c. Commensurable
d. Concurrent

58. _____ are three or more lines that intersect at a single point.
   a. Mathematical coincidence
   b. Concurrent lines
   c. Handwaving
   d. Connectedness

59. In mathematics, a _____ is, informally, an infinitely vast and infinitely thin sheet. _____s may be thought of as objects in some higher dimensional space, or they may be considered without any outside space, as in the setting of Euclidean geometry
   a. Bandwidth
   b. Group
   c. Blocking
   d. Plane

60. The _____ is the distance around a closed curve. _____ is a kind of perimeter.

The _____ of a circle is the length around it.

   a. Compactness measure of a shape
   b. Circumference
   c. Flatness
   d. Brascamp-Lieb inequality

61. _____ is the likelihood or chance that something is the case or will happen. Theoretical _____ is used extensively in areas such as statistics, mathematics, science and philosophy to draw conclusions about the likelihood of potential events and the underlying mechanics of complex systems.

The word _____ does not have a consistent direct definition.

   a. Statistical significance
   b. Standardized moment
   c. Probability
   d. Discrete random variable

62. _____ is an adjective meaning contiguous, adjoining or abutting.

In geometry, _____ is when sides meet to make an angle.

In trigonometry the _____ side of a right angled triangle is the cathetus next to the angle in question.

   a. Affine geometry
   b. Adjacent
   c. Ordered geometry
   d. Ambient space

63. In geometry, _____ are angles that have a common ray coming out of the vertex going between two other rays. In other words, they are angles that are side by side, or adjacent.

An angle with a ray connected to a common point down the center.

   a. A Mathematical Theory of Communication
   b. Elliptic geometry
   c. Erlangen Program
   d. Adjacent angles

Chapter 12. GEOMETRIC SHAPES

64. _____ is a temperature scale that is named after the German physicist Daniel Gabriel _____, who proposed it in 1724.

In this scale, the freezing point of water is 32 degrees _____ and the boiling point 212 °F, placing the boiling and freezing points of water exactly 180 degrees apart. A degree on the _____ scale is 1/180th part of the interval between the ice point and the boiling point.

a. 2-3 heap
b. 120-cell
c. Fahrenheit
d. 1-center problem

65. In mathematics the concept of a _____ generalizes notions such as 'length', 'area', and 'volume'. Informally, given some base set, a '_____' is any consistent assignment of 'sizes' to the subsets of the base set. Depending on the application, the 'size' of a subset may be interpreted as its physical size, the amount of something that lies within the subset, or the probability that some random process will yield a result within the subset.

a. Lattice
b. Measure
c. Congruent
d. Cusp

66. An angle equal to two right angles is called a _____ (equal to 180 degrees).
a. Householder transformation
b. Theorem
c. Loomis-Whitney inequality
d. Straight angle

67. A pair of angles are said to be _____ if they share the same vertex and are bounded by the same pair of lines but are opposite to each other. They are also congruent.
a. Line segment
b. Reflection symmetry
c. Hinge theorem
d. Vertical angles

68. An angle smaller than a right angle is called an _____ (less than 90 degrees).
a. Euclidean geometry
b. Ultraparallel theorem
c. Acute Angle
d. Integral geometry

69. A pair of angles are complementary if the sum of their measures add up to 90 degrees.

If the two _____ are adjacent (i.e. have a common vertex and share a side, but do not have any interior points in common) their non-shared sides form a right angle.

In Euclidean geometry, the two acute angles in a right triangle are complementary, because there are 180>° in a triangle and 90>° have been accounted for by the right angle.

a. Hypotenuse
b. Complementary angles
c. Conway polyhedron notation
d. Quincunx

70. _____ are formed when a given transversal line crosses two coplanar lines. The _____ are not necessarily congruent. In the event that the _____ are congruent, these angles can be used to determine the degrees of the other angles of the parallel lines.

Chapter 12. GEOMETRIC SHAPES

a. Corresponding angles
b. Conformal connection
c. Brocard circle
d. Prismatic pentagonal tiling

71. A pair of angles is _____ if their measurements add up to 180 degrees. If the two _____ angles are adjacent their non-shared sides form a straight line. The supplement of 135 would be 45.
  a. Dense
  b. FISH
  c. Cylinder
  d. Supplementary

72. In combinatorial mathematics, given a collection C of sets, a _____ is a set containing exactly one element from each member of the collection: it is a section of the quotient map induced by the collection. If the original sets are not disjoint, there are several different definitions. One variation is that there is a bijection f from the _____ to C such that x is an element of f
  a. Combinadic
  b. Combinatorial design
  c. Transversal
  d. Heawood number

73. A _____ is a 2D geometric symbolic representation of information according to some visualization technique. Sometimes, the technique uses a 3D visualization which is then projected onto the 2D surface. The word graph is sometimes used as a synonym for _____.
  a. 120-cell
  b. 2-3 heap
  c. 1-center problem
  d. Diagram

74. In mathematics, a _____ is a statement that can be proved on the basis of explicitly stated or previously agreed assumptions.
  a. Boolean function
  b. Disjunction introduction
  c. Logical value
  d. Theorem

75. An _____ is a triangle that has one internal angle larger than 90°
  a. A chemical equation
  b. A Mathematical Theory of Communication
  c. Isotomic conjugate
  d. Obtuse triangle

76. A _____ is a building where the upper surfaces are triangular and converge on one point. The base of _____s are usually quadrilateral or trilateral, meaning that a _____ usually has four or five faces. A _____'s design, with the majority of the weight closer to the ground, means that less material higher up on the _____ will be pushing down from above.
  a. 1-center problem
  b. Pyramid
  c. 2-3 heap
  d. 120-cell

77. A _____ or tiling of the plane is a collection of plane figures that fills the plane with no overlaps and no gaps. One may also speak of _____s of the parts of the plane or of other surfaces. Generalizations to higher dimensions are also possible.
  a. Directional symmetry
  b. Symmetry breaking
  c. Molecular symmetry
  d. Tessellation

78. In geometry, a _____ is a polygon with seven sides and seven angles. In a regular _____, in which all sides and all angles are equal, the sides meet at an angle of 5π/7 radians, 128.5714286 degrees. Its Schläfli symbol is {7}.

Chapter 12. GEOMETRIC SHAPES

a. Hexagon
b. Pentagon
c. Heptadecagon
d. Heptagon

79. In geometry, a _____ is a polygon with six edges and six vertices. A regular _____ has Schläfli symbol {6}.

The internal angles of a regular _____ are all 120° and the _____ has 720 degrees.

a. Polygonal curve
b. Polygonal chain
c. Hexagon
d. Decagon

80. In geometry, a _____ is a set of points in space described by their relative positions. They can be described by their use in polytopes.

For example a square _____ is understood to mean four points in a plane, equal distance and angles from a center point.

a. Hendecagram
b. Mandart inellipse
c. Vertex arrangement
d. Kobon triangle problem

81. In the mathematical area of order theory, every partially ordered set P gives rise to a _____ partially ordered set which is often denoted by P^{op} or P^d. This _____ order P^{op} is defined to be the set with the inverse order. It is easy to see that this construction, which can be depicted by flipping the Hasse diagram for P upside down, will indeed yield a partially ordered set.

a. Contraction mapping
b. Context-sensitive language
c. Christofides heuristics
d. Dual

82. In geometry a _____ is, broadly speaking, the figure exposed when a corner of a polyhedron or polytope is sliced off.

Take some vertex of a polyhedron. Mark a point somewhere along each connected edge.

a. Prismatic surface
b. First Hurwitz triplet
c. Projective geometry
d. Vertex figure

83. In mathematics, _____ are two-dimensional manifolds or surfaces that are perfectly flat.
a. 120-cell
b. 2-3 heap
c. 1-center problem
d. Planes

84. In geometry, the angle between two planes is called their _____ or torsion angle. Figure 1: _____ angle of three vectors, defined as an exterior spherical angle. The longer and shorter black segments are arcs of the great circles passing through b_1 and b_2 and through b_2 and b_3, respectively. Figure 2: _____ angle defined by three bond vectors connecting four atoms. Figure 3: _____ angle defined by three bond vectors connecting four atoms.

Chapter 12. GEOMETRIC SHAPES

a. Drag count
b. Drag equation
c. 1-center problem
d. Dihedral

85. _____ or _____ lines lie on different planes. They are neither parallel nor intersecting.

- In geometry, straight lines in a space referred to as _____ if they are neither parallel nor intersecting.
- In statistics, _____ is sometimes used as an alternative term to skewness to refer to the degree of asymmetry of a distribution. It can mean distortion in a positive or negative direction.

- In parallel transmission, the difference in arrival time of bits transmitted at the same time.

- For data recorded on multichannel magnetic tape, the difference between reading times of bits recorded in a single transverse line.

Nte: _____ is usually interpreted to mean the difference in reading times between bits recorded on the tracks at the extremities, or edges, of the tape.

a. Common operator notation
b. P-wave
c. Genus
d. Skew

86. The term _____ refers to the central sense organ complex, for those animals that have one, normally on the ventral surface of the head and can depending on the definition in the human case, include the hair, forehead, eyebrow, eyes, nose, ears, cheeks, mouth, lips, philtrum, teeth, skin, and chin. The _____ has uses of expression, appearance, and identity amongst others.It also has different senses like smelling, tasting, hearing, and seeing.

Caricatures often exaggerate facial features to make a _____ more easily recognized in association with a pronounced portion of the _____ of the individual in question--for example, a caricature of Osama bin Laden might focus on his facial hair and nose; a caricature of George W. Bush might enlarge his ears to the size of an elephant¢s; a caricature of Jay Leno may pronounce his head and chin; and a caricature of Mick Jagger might enlarge his lips.

a. 120-cell
b. 1-center problem
c. 2-3 heap
d. Face

87. In geometry, _____ are associated into pairs called duals, where the vertices of one correspond to the faces of the other. The dual of the dual is the original polyhedron. The dual of a polyhedron with equivalent vertices is one with equivalent faces, and of one with equivalent edges is another with equivalent edges.
a. Polyhedra
b. Disk
c. Coherence
d. Gravity waves

88. In mathematics, _____ and undefined are used to explain whether or not expressions have meaningful, sensible, and unambiguous values. Not all branches of mathematics come to the same conclusion.

The following expressions are undefined in all contexts, but remarks in the analysis section may apply.

Chapter 12. GEOMETRIC SHAPES

  a. Plugging in
  b. Defined
  c. LHS
  d. Toy model

89. In geometry, an _____ is a descriptive label for a visual singular highest or most distant point or vertex in an isosceles triangle, pyramid or cone, usually contrasting with the opposite side called the base. For an isosceles triangle the _____ is the vertex where the two sides of equal length meet. .
  a. Epigraph
  b. Emphasis
  c. Apex
  d. Amortization

90. In geometry, a _____ is a convex regular polyhedron. These are the three-dimensional analogs of the convex regular polygons. There are precisely five such figures.
  a. 2-3 heap
  b. 1-center problem
  c. 120-cell
  d. Platonic solid

91. In mathematics, the _____s are analogs of the ordinary trigonometric functions. The basic _____s are the hyperbolic sine 'sinh', and the hyperbolic cosine 'cosh', from which are derived the hyperbolic tangent 'tanh', etc., in analogy to the derived trigonometric functions. The inverse _____ are the area hyperbolic sine 'arsinh' (also called 'asinh', or sometimes by the misnomer of 'arcsinh') and so on.
  a. Rectangular function
  b. Hyperbolic function
  c. Square root
  d. Heaviside step function

92. A _____ is a three-dimensional geometric shape that tapers smoothly from a flat, round base to a point called the apex or vertex. More precisely, it is the solid figure bounded by a plane base and the surface formed by the locus of all straight line segments joining the apex to the perimeter of the base. The term '_____' sometimes refers just to the surface of this solid figure, or just to the lateral surface.
  a. Characteristic
  b. Cone
  c. Gravity waves
  d. Blocking

93. In mathematics and in the sciences, a _____ (plural: _____e, formulæ or _____s) is a concise way of expressing information symbolically (as in a mathematical or chemical _____), or a general relationship between quantities. One of many famous _____e is Albert Einstein's $E = mc^2$ (see special relativity

In mathematics, a _____ is a key to solve an equation with variables. For example, the problem of determining the volume of a sphere is one that requires a significant amount of integral calculus to solve.

  a. 2-3 heap
  b. 1-center problem
  c. 120-cell
  d. Formula

94. A _____ is often defined as a geometric object with flat faces and straight edges .

This definition of a _____ is not very precise, and to a modern mathematician is quite unsatisfactory. Grünbaum observed that:

The Original Sin in the theory of polyhedra goes back to Euclid, and through Kepler, Poinsot, Cauchy and many others ...

a. 2-3 heap
b. 1-center problem
c. Polyhedron
d. 120-cell

95. A _____ is any polyhedron with twelve faces, but usually a regular _____ is meant: a Platonic solid composed of twelve regular pentagonal faces, with three meeting at each vertex. It has twenty vertices and thirty edges. Its dual polyhedron is the icosahedron.
   a. 1-center problem
   b. 2-3 heap
   c. 120-cell
   d. Dodecahedron

96. A _____ is a polyhedron with six faces. A regular _____, with all its faces square, is a cube.

There many kinds of _____, some topologically similar to the cube, and some not.

   a. Wythoff construction
   b. Parallelepiped
   c. Hoberman sphere
   d. Hexahedron

97. An _____ is a polyhedron with eight faces. A regular _____ is a Platonic solid composed of eight equilateral triangles, four of which meet at each vertex.

The _____'s symmetry group is O_h, of order 48.

   a. A posteriori
   b. A Mathematical Theory of Communication
   c. A chemical equation
   d. Octahedron

98. A _____ is a polyhedron composed of four triangular faces, three of which meet at each vertex. A regular _____ is one in which the four triangles are regular, or 'equilateral', and is one of the Platonic solids.

The _____ is one kind of pyramid, which is a polyhedron with a flat polygon base and triangular faces connecting the base to a common point.

   a. 2-3 heap
   b. Tetrahedron
   c. 120-cell
   d. 1-center problem

99. In mathematics, a _____ is a quadric surface, with the following equation in Cartesian coordinates: $(x/_a)^2 + (y/_b)^2 = 1$.
   a. Derivative algebra
   b. Cylinder
   c. Free
   d. Discontinuity

100. _____ is a three-dimensional geometric shape formed by straight lines through a fixed point vertex to the points of a fixed curve directrix.
   a. 2-3 heap
   b. Right circular cone
   c. 1-center problem
   d. 120-cell

101. In common usage, a cylinder is taken to mean a finite section of a _____ with its ends closed to form two circular surfaces, as in the figure (right.) If the cylinder has a radius r and length (height) h, then its volume is given by

$$V = \pi r^2 h$$

and its surface area is:

- the area of the top (πr^2) +
- the area of the bottom (πr^2) +
- the area of the side $(2\pi r h)$.

Therefore without the top or bottom (lateral area), the surface area is

$$A = 2\pi r h.$$

With the top and bottom, the surface area is

$$A = 2\pi r^2 + 2\pi r h = 2\pi r(r + h).$$

For a given volume, the cylinder with the smallest surface area has h = 2r. For a given surface area, the cylinder with the largest volume has h = 2r, i.e. the cylinder fits in a cube (height = diameter.)

Cylindric sections are the intersections of cylinders with planes.

a. 120-cell
c. Right circular cylinder

b. 2-3 heap
d. 1-center problem

102. In common usage, a cylinder is taken to mean a finite section of a right _____ with its ends closed to form two circular surfaces, as in the figure (right.) If the cylinder has a radius r and length (height) h, then its volume is given by

$$V = \pi r^2 h$$

and its surface area is:

- the area of the top (πr^2) +
- the area of the bottom (πr^2) +
- the area of the side $(2\pi r h)$.

Therefore without the top or bottom (lateral area), the surface area is

$$A = 2\pi r h.$$

Chapter 12. GEOMETRIC SHAPES

With the top and bottom, the surface area is

$$A = 2\pi r^2 + 2\pi rh = 2\pi r(r+h).$$

For a given volume, the cylinder with the smallest surface area has h = 2r. For a given surface area, the cylinder with the largest volume has h = 2r, i.e. the cylinder fits in a cube (height = diameter.)

Cylindric sections are the intersections of cylinders with planes.

a. 1-center problem
c. 2-3 heap
b. 120-cell
d. Circular Cylinder

103. In mathematics, the concept of a curve tries to capture the intuitive idea of a geometrical one-dimensional and continuous object. A simple example is the circle. In everyday use of the term 'curve', a straight line is not _____, but in mathematical parlance curves include straight lines and line segments.
   a. Witch of Maria Agnesi
   c. Hypocycloid
   b. Cissoid of Diocles
   d. Curved

104. The _____ is an Archimedean solid. It has 6 regular octagonal faces, 8 regular triangular faces, 24 vertices and 36 edges.

The area A and the volume V of a _____ of edge length a are:

$$A = 2(6 + 6\sqrt{2} + \sqrt{3})a^2 \approx 32.4346644a^2$$
$$V = \frac{1}{3}(21 + 14\sqrt{2})a^3 \approx 13.5996633a^3.$$

The following Cartesian coordinates define the vertices of a truncated hexahedron centered at the origin with edge length 2ξ:

where ξ = $\sqrt{2} - 1$

Compare:

It shares the vertex arrangement with three uniform star polyhedrons:

- Spinning _____
- Cube-connected cycles, a family of graphs that includes the skeleton of the _____

a. Truncated dodecahedron
b. Truncated octahedron
c. Rhombicuboctahedron
d. Truncated Cube

105. A _____ is a symmetrical geometrical object. In non-mathematical usage, the term is used to refer either to a round ball or to its two-dimensional surface. In mathematics, a _____ is the set of all points in three-dimensional space which are at distance r from a fixed point of that space, where r is a positive real number called the radius of the _____.
a. Sphere
b. Differential geometry of curves
c. Lie derivative
d. Differentiable manifold

Chapter 13. MEASUREMENT

1. The _____ of a material is defined as its mass per unit volume:

$$\rho = \frac{m}{V}$$

Different materials usually have different densities, so _____ is an important concept regarding buoyancy, metal purity and packaging.

In some cases _____ is expressed as the dimensionless quantities specific gravity or relative _____, in which case it is expressed in multiples of the _____ of some other standard material, usually water or air.

In a well-known story, Archimedes was given the task of determining whether King Hiero's goldsmith was embezzling gold during the manufacture of a wreath dedicated to the gods and replacing it with another, cheaper alloy.

a. 120-cell
b. 2-3 heap
c. 1-center problem
d. Density

2. _____ is a conceptual tool often applied in physics, chemistry, engineering, mathematics and statistics to understand physical situations involving a mix of different kinds of physical quantities. It is routinely used by physical scientists and engineers to check the plausibility of derived equations and computations. It is also used to form reasonable hypotheses about complex physical situations that can be tested by experiment or by more developed theories of the phenomena.

a. 1-center problem
b. 120-cell
c. 2-3 heap
d. Dimensional Analysis

3. In cryptography, _____ is a pseudorandom number generator and a stream cipher designed by Robert Jenkins to be cryptographically secure. The name is an acronym for Indirection, Shift, Accumulate, Add, and Count.

The _____ algorithm has similarities with RC4.

a. Order
b. Introduction
c. Imputation
d. Isaac

4. _____ was a German polymath who wrote primarily in Latin and French.

He occupies an equally grand place in both the history of philosophy and the history of mathematics. He invented infinitesimal calculus independently of Newton, and his notation is the one in general use since then.

a. Raymond Merrill Smullyan
b. Harry Hinsley
c. Michel Rolle
d. Gottfried Wilhelm Leibniz

5. The framework of quantum mechanics requires a careful definition of _____, and a thorough discussion of its practical and philosophical implications.

_____ is viewed in different ways in the many interpretations of quantum mechanics; however, despite the considerable philosophical differences, they almost universally agree on the practical question of what results from a routine quantum-physics laboratory _____. To describe this, a simple framework to use is the Copenhagen interpretation, and it will be implicitly used in this section; the utility of this approach has been verified countless times, and all other interpretations are necessarily constructed so as to give the same quantitative predictions as this in almost every case.

a. 1-center problem
c. Measurement
b. Dynamic range
d. Fundamental units

6. The _____ (symbol: N) is the SI derived unit of force, named after Isaac _____ in recognition of his work on classical mechanics.

The _____ is the unit of force derived in the SI system; it is equal to the amount of force required to accelerate a mass of one kilogram at a rate of one meter per second per second. Algebraically:

$$1\ N = 1\ \frac{kg \cdot m}{s^2}.$$

- 1 N is the force of Earth's gravity on an object with a mass of about 102 g ($1/_{9.8}$ kg) (such as a small apple.)
- On Earth's surface, a mass of 1 kg exerts a force of approximately 9.80665 N [down] (or 1 kgf.) The approximation of 1 kg corresponding to 10 N is sometimes used as a rule of thumb in everyday life and in engineering.
- The force of Earth's gravity on a human being with a mass of 70 kg is approximately 687 N.
- The dot product of force and distance is mechanical work. Thus, in SI units, a force of 1 N exerted over a distance of 1 m is 1 N·m of work. The Work-Energy Theorem states that the work done on a body is equal to the change in energy of the body. 1 N·m = 1 J (joule), the SI unit of energy.
- It is common to see forces expressed in kilonewtons or kN, where 1 kN = 1 000 N.

a. 1-center problem
c. Newton
b. 120-cell
d. 2-3 heap

7. _____ is a special mathematical relationship between two quantities. Two quantities are called proportional if they vary in such a way that one of the quantities is a constant multiple of the other, or equivalently if they have a constant ratio.
a. Depth
c. Compression
b. Discontinuity
d. Proportionality

8. In mathematics, a _____ is a number which can be expressed as a ratio of two integers. Non-integer _____s are usually written as the vulgar fraction $\frac{a}{b}$, where b is not zero. a is called the numerator, and b the denominator.

Chapter 13. MEASUREMENT

a. Minkowski distance
b. Tally marks
c. Pre-algebra
d. Rational number

9. In game theory, a player's _____ in a game is a complete plan of action for whatever situation might arise; this fully determines the player's behaviour. A player's _____ will determine the action the player will take at any stage of the game, for every possible history of play up to that stage.

A _____ profile is a set of strategies for each player which fully specifies all actions in a game.

a. Strategy
b. Correlated equilibrium
c. Sir Philip Sidney game
d. Matching pennies

10. The _____ is a decimalised system of measurement. It exists in several variations, with different choices of base units, though the choice of base units does not affect its day-to-day use. Over the last two centuries, different variants have been considered the _____.
a. 1-center problem
b. George Dantzig
c. Metric system
d. Nonlinear system

11. In mathematics the concept of a _____ generalizes notions such as 'length', 'area', and 'volume'. Informally, given some base set, a '_____' is any consistent assignment of 'sizes' to the subsets of the base set. Depending on the application, the 'size' of a subset may be interpreted as its physical size, the amount of something that lies within the subset, or the probability that some random process will yield a result within the subset.
a. Lattice
b. Cusp
c. Congruent
d. Measure

12. In mathematics, the _____ or Pythagoras' theorem is a relation in Euclidean geometry among the three sides of a right triangle. The theorem is named after the Greek mathematician Pythagoras, who by tradition is credited with its discovery and proof, although it is often argued that knowledge of the theory predates him.. The theorem is as follows:

In any right triangle, the area of the square whose side is the hypotenuse is equal to the sum of the areas of the squares whose sides are the two legs.

a. 120-cell
b. 1-center problem
c. Pythagorean theorem
d. 2-3 heap

13. In mathematics and in the sciences, a _____ (plural: _____e, formulæ or _____s) is a concise way of expressing information symbolically (as in a mathematical or chemical _____), or a general relationship between quantities. One of many famous _____e is Albert Einstein's $E = mc^2$ (see special relativity

In mathematics, a _____ is a key to solve an equation with variables. For example, the problem of determining the volume of a sphere is one that requires a significant amount of integral calculus to solve.

a. 1-center problem
b. Formula
c. 2-3 heap
d. 120-cell

Chapter 13. MEASUREMENT

14. In mathematics, a _____ is a statement that can be proved on the basis of explicitly stated or previously agreed assumptions.
   a. Disjunction introduction
   b. Boolean function
   c. Logical value
   d. Theorem

15. _____ is a quantity expressing the two-dimensional size of a defined part of a surface, typically a region bounded by a closed curve. The term surface _____ refers to the total _____ of the exposed surface of a 3-dimensional solid, such as the sum of the _____s of the exposed sides of a polyhedron. _____ is an important invariant in the differential geometry of surfaces.
   a. A posteriori
   b. A chemical equation
   c. A Mathematical Theory of Communication
   d. Area

16. The _____ of any solid, plasma, vacuum or theoretical object is how much three-dimensional space it occupies, often quantified numerically. One-dimensional figures and two-dimensional shapes are assigned zero _____ in the three-dimensional space. _____ is presented as ml or cm^3.

   _____s of straight-edged and circular shapes are calculated using arithmetic formulae.

   a. Stress-energy tensor
   b. Cauchy momentum equation
   c. Thermodynamic limit
   d. Volume

17. _____ is a stream cipher submitted to eSTREAM in 2004 by Martin Hell, Thomas Johansson and Willi Meier. It has been selected for the final eSTREAM portfolio for Profile 2 by the eSTREAM project. _____ is designed primarily for restricted hardware environments.
   a. SNOW
   b. MULTI-S01
   c. Phelix
   d. Grain

18. _____ is one of the principal states of matter. A _____ is a fluid that has the particles loose and can freely form a distinct surface at the boundaries of its bulk material. The surface is a free surface where the _____ is not constrained by a container.
   a. 120-cell
   b. 2-3 heap
   c. 1-center problem
   d. Liquid

19. In the physical sciences, _____ is a measurement of the gravitational force acting on an object. Near the surface of the Earth, the acceleration due to gravity is approximately constant; this means that an object's _____ is roughly proportional to its mass.

   In commerce and in many other applications, _____ means the same as mass as that term is used in physics.

   a. 120-cell
   b. 2-3 heap
   c. 1-center problem
   d. Weight

20. The _____ is the distance around a closed curve. _____ is a kind of perimeter.

   The _____ of a circle is the length around it.

Chapter 13. MEASUREMENT

a. Flatness
b. Compactness measure of a shape
c. Brascamp-Lieb inequality
d. Circumference

21. _____ is a temperature scale that is named after the German physicist Daniel Gabriel _____, who proposed it in 1724.

In this scale, the freezing point of water is 32 degrees _____ and the boiling point 212 °F, placing the boiling and freezing points of water exactly 180 degrees apart. A degree on the _____ scale is 1/180th part of the interval between the ice point and the boiling point.

a. 120-cell
b. Fahrenheit
c. 1-center problem
d. 2-3 heap

22. In mathematics and computer science, _____ (also base-16, hexa or base, of 16. It uses sixteen distinct symbols, most often the symbols 0-9 to represent values zero to nine, and A, B, C, D, E, F (or a through f) to represent values ten to fifteen.

Its primary use is as a human friendly representation of binary coded values, so it is often used in digital electronics and computer engineering.

a. Tetradecimal
b. Radix
c. Hexadecimal
d. Factoradic

23. A _____ is a type of affix attached to a stem which modifies the meaning of that stem.

The word '_____' is itself made up of the stem fix, and the _____ pre-, both of which are derived from Latin roots.

- English _____es
- _____es and suffixes in Hebrew

a. 1-center problem
b. 120-cell
c. 2-3 heap
d. Prefix

24. The _____ is the derived unit of energy in the International System of Units. It is defined as:

$$1\,\mathrm{J} = 1\,\mathrm{kg} \cdot \frac{\mathrm{m}^2}{\mathrm{s}^2}$$

One _____ is the amount of energy required to perform the following actions:

- The work done by a force of one newton travelling through a distance of one meter;
- The work required to move an electric charge of one coulomb through an electrical potential difference of one volt; or one coulomb volt, with the symbol CÂ·V;
- The work done to produce power of one watt continuously for one second; or one watt second, with the symbol WÂ·s. Thus a kilowatt hour is 3,600,000 _____ s or 3.6 megajoules;
- The kinetic energy of a 2 kg mass moving at a velocity of 1 m/s. The energy is linear in the mass but quadratic in the velocity, being given by $E = 1/2 mv^2$;

a. 1-center problem
b. 2-3 heap
c. Joule
d. 120-cell

25. The _____ is the length of the line that bounds an area In the special case where the area is circular, the _____ is known as the circumference.
    a. Multilateration
    b. Reflection symmetry
    c. Concyclic
    d. Perimeter

26. In geometry, a _____ is defined as a quadrilateral where all four of its angles are right angles.
    a. Rectangle
    b. Cantor-Dedekind axiom
    c. Polytope
    d. Point group in two dimensions

27. A _____ is a flying tethered object that depends upon the tension of a tethering system. The necessary lift that makes the _____ wing fly is generated when air flows over and under the _____ 's wing, producing low pressure above the wing and high pressure below it. This deflection also generates horizontal drag along the direction of the wind.
    a. 1-center problem
    b. 120-cell
    c. 2-3 heap
    d. Kite

28. A _____ is a simple shape of Euclidean geometry consisting of those points in a plane which are at a constant distance, called the radius, from a fixed point, called the center. A _____ with center A is sometimes denoted by the symbol A.

A chord of a _____ is a line segment whose two endpoints lie on the _____ .

   a. Circular segment
   b. Malfatti circles
   c. Circumcircle
   d. Circle

29. In geometry a _____ is traditionally a plane figure that is bounded by a closed path or circuit, composed of a finite sequence of straight line segments. These segments are called its edges or sides, and the points where two edges meet are the _____ 's vertices or corners. The interior of the _____ is sometimes called its body.
    a. Polygon
    b. Regular polygon
    c. Polygonal curve
    d. Parallelogon

Chapter 13. MEASUREMENT

30. In geometry, a _____ is a quadrilateral with two sets of parallel sides. The opposite sides of a _____ are of equal length, and the opposite angles of a _____ are congruent. The three-dimensional counterpart of a _____ is a parallelepiped.
   a. 120-cell
   b. 2-3 heap
   c. Parallelogram
   d. 1-center problem

31. In geometry, a _____, or rhomb is an equilateral parallelogram. In other words, it is a four-sided polygon in which every side has the same length.

The _____ is often casually called a diamond, after the diamonds suit in playing cards, or a lozenge, because those shapes are rhombi, although rhombi are not necessarily diamonds or lozenges.

   a. 1-center problem
   b. Rhombus
   c. 2-3 heap
   d. 120-cell

32. In mathematics, specifically in topology, a _____ is a two-dimensional manifold. The most familiar examples are those that arise as the boundaries of solid objects in ordinary three-dimensional Euclidean space, EÂ³. On the other hand, there are also more exotic _____s, that are so 'contorted' that they cannot be embedded in three-dimensional space at all.
   a. Homoeoid
   b. Standard torus
   c. Cross-cap
   d. Surface

33. A _____ is one of the basic shapes of geometry: a polygon with three corners or vertices and three sides or edges which are line segments. A _____ with vertices A, B, and C is denoted ABC.

In Euclidean geometry any three non-collinear points determine a unique _____ and a unique plane.

   a. 1-center problem
   b. Fuhrmann circle
   c. Kepler triangle
   d. Triangle

34. A _____ is a mathematical manipulative often used to explore basic concepts in plane geometry such as perimeter, area or the characteristics of triangles and other polygons. Consisting of a physical board with a certain number of nails half driven in, in a symmetrical square five-by-five array, students are encouraged to place rubber bands around the pegs to model various geometric concepts or to solve other mathematical puzzles. Two-dimensional representations of the _____ may be applied to ordinary paper using rubber stamps or special '_____ paper' with diagrams of _____s may be used to help capture a student's explanations of the concept they have discovered or illustrated on the _____.
   a. 1-center problem
   b. Cuisenaire rods
   c. Van Hiele levels
   d. Geoboard

35. _____ is the measurement of vertical distance, but has two meanings in common use. It can either indicate how 'tall' something is, or how 'high up' it is. For example one could say 'That is a tall building', or 'That airplane is high up in the sky'.
   a. 2-3 heap
   b. 120-cell
   c. 1-center problem
   d. Height

Chapter 13. MEASUREMENT

36. A _____ is a three-dimensional geometric shape that tapers smoothly from a flat, round base to a point called the apex or vertex. More precisely, it is the solid figure bounded by a plane base and the surface formed by the locus of all straight line segments joining the apex to the perimeter of the base. The term '_____' sometimes refers just to the surface of this solid figure, or just to the lateral surface.

   a. Gravity waves
   b. Characteristic
   c. Blocking
   d. Cone

37. A _____ or a trapezium is a quadrilateral that has at least one pair of parallel lines for sides.

Some authors define it as a quadrilateral having exactly one pair of parallel sides, so as to exclude parallelograms, which otherwise would be regarded as a special type of _____, but most mathematicians use the inclusive definition.

In North America, the term trapezium is used to refer to a quadrilateral with no parallel sides.

   a. Lozenge
   b. Trapezium
   c. Rhomboid
   d. Trapezoid

38. A _____ is the longest side of a right triangle, the side opposite of the right angle. The length of the _____ of a right triangle can be found using the Pythagorean theorem, which states that the square of the length of the _____ equals the sum of the squares of the lengths of the two other sides.

For example, if one of the other sides has a length of 3 meters and the other has a length of 4 m.

   a. Golden angle
   b. Reflection symmetry
   c. Concyclic points
   d. Hypotenuse

39. In a right triangle, the cathetusoriginally from the Greek word KÎ¬θετος, plural catheti

   - 1 Generally
   - 2 References
   - 3 See also
   - 4 External links

In a wider sense, a _____ is any line falling perpendicularly on another line or a surface. Such a line is more commonly known as a surface normal.

   a. Face diagonal
   b. Central angle
   c. Line segment
   d. Cathetus

40. The _____ is πr^2 when the circle has radius r. Here the symbol π denotes, as usual, the constant ratio of the circumference of a circle to its diameter.

Modern mathematics can obtain the area using the methods of integral calculus or its more sophisticated offspring, real analysis.

Chapter 13. MEASUREMENT

a. A Mathematical Theory of Communication
b. A chemical equation
c. Ultraparallel theorem
d. Area of a circle

41. In mathematics, an _____ is a statement about the relative size or order of two objects, or about whether they are the same or not

- The notation a < b means that a is less than b.
- The notation a > b means that a is greater than b.
- The notation a ≠ b means that a is not equal to b, but does not say that one is bigger than the other or even that they can be compared in size.

In all these cases, a is not equal to b, hence, '_____'.

These relations are known as strict _____

- The notation a ≤ b means that a is less than or equal to b;
- The notation a ≥ b means that a is greater than or equal to b;

An additional use of the notation is to show that one quantity is much greater than another, normally by several orders of magnitude.

- The notation a << b means that a is much less than b.
- The notation a >> b means that a is much greater than b.

If the sense of the _____ is the same for all values of the variables for which its members are defined, then the _____ is called an 'absolute' or 'unconditional' _____. If the sense of an _____ holds only for certain values of the variables involved, but is reversed or destroyed for other values of the variables, it is called a conditional _____.

An _____ may appear unsolvable because it only states whether a number is larger or smaller than another number; but it is possible to apply the same operations for equalities to inequalities. For example, to find x for the _____ 10x > 23 one would divide 23 by 10.

a. A Mathematical Theory of Communication
b. A posteriori
c. A chemical equation
d. Inequality

42. In mathematics, the _____ states that for any triangle, the length of a given side must be less than the sum of the other two sides but greater than the difference between the two sides.

In Euclidean geometry and some other geometries this is a theorem. In the Euclidean case, in both the less than or equal to and greater than or equal to statements, equality occurs only if the triangle has a 180° angle and two 0° angles, as shown in the bottom example in the image to the right.

Chapter 13. MEASUREMENT

    a. Rearrangement inequality
    b. Greater than
    c. Minkowski inequality
    d. Triangle Inequality

43. _____ objects share the same center, axis or origin with one inside the other. Circles, tubes, cylindrical shafts, disks, and spheres may be _____ to one another. _____ objects do not necessarily have the same radius.
    a. Surface area
    b. Gyroid
    c. Covering radius
    d. Concentric

44. A _____ is a symmetrical geometrical object. In non-mathematical usage, the term is used to refer either to a round ball or to its two-dimensional surface. In mathematics, a _____ is the set of all points in three-dimensional space which are at distance r from a fixed point of that space, where r is a positive real number called the radius of the _____.
    a. Differentiable manifold
    b. Lie derivative
    c. Sphere
    d. Differential geometry of curves

45. _____ is how much exposed area an object has. It is expressed in square units. If an object has flat faces, its _____ can be calculated by adding together the areas of its faces.
    a. Reflection group
    b. Surface area
    c. Relative dimension
    d. Compactness measure of a shape

46. In mathematics, _____ and undefined are used to explain whether or not expressions have meaningful, sensible, and unambiguous values. Not all branches of mathematics come to the same conclusion.

The following expressions are undefined in all contexts, but remarks in the analysis section may apply.

    a. Plugging in
    b. LHS
    c. Defined
    d. Toy model

47. In geometry, the _____ of a solid is the face or surface of the solid on its sides. That is, any face or surface that is not a base.
    a. Concentric
    b. Birational geometry
    c. Circumference
    d. Lateral Surface

48. In mathematics, a _____ is a quadric surface, with the following equation in Cartesian coordinates: $(x/a)^2 + (y/b)^2 = 1$.
    a. Derivative algebra
    b. Discontinuity
    c. Free
    d. Cylinder

49. In common usage, a cylinder is taken to mean a finite section of a _____ with its ends closed to form two circular surfaces, as in the figure (right.) If the cylinder has a radius r and length (height) h, then its volume is given by

$$V = \pi r^2 h$$

and its surface area is:

- the area of the top (πr^2) +
- the area of the bottom (πr^2) +
- the area of the side $(2\pi r h)$.

Therefore without the top or bottom (lateral area), the surface area is

$$A = 2\pi r h.$$

With the top and bottom, the surface area is

$$A = 2\pi r^2 + 2\pi r h = 2\pi r(r + h).$$

For a given volume, the cylinder with the smallest surface area has h = 2r. For a given surface area, the cylinder with the largest volume has h = 2r, i.e. the cylinder fits in a cube (height = diameter.)

Cylindric sections are the intersections of cylinders with planes.

a. 1-center problem
c. 2-3 heap

b. 120-cell
d. Right circular cylinder

50. In mathematics, the _____s are analogs of the ordinary trigonometric functions. The basic _____s are the hyperbolic sine 'sinh', and the hyperbolic cosine 'cosh', from which are derived the hyperbolic tangent 'tanh', etc., in analogy to the derived trigonometric functions. The inverse _____ are the area hyperbolic sine 'arsinh' (also called 'asinh', or sometimes by the misnomer of 'arcsinh') and so on.

a. Heaviside step function
c. Rectangular function

b. Square root
d. Hyperbolic function

51. In common usage, a cylinder is taken to mean a finite section of a right _____ with its ends closed to form two circular surfaces, as in the figure (right.) If the cylinder has a radius r and length (height) h, then its volume is given by

$$V = \pi r^2 h$$

and its surface area is:

- the area of the top (πr^2) +
- the area of the bottom (πr^2) +
- the area of the side $(2\pi r h)$.

Therefore without the top or bottom (lateral area), the surface area is

$$A = 2\pi rh.$$

With the top and bottom, the surface area is

$$A = 2\pi r^2 + 2\pi rh = 2\pi r(r + h).$$

For a given volume, the cylinder with the smallest surface area has h = 2r. For a given surface area, the cylinder with the largest volume has h = 2r, i.e. the cylinder fits in a cube (height = diameter.)

Cylindric sections are the intersections of cylinders with planes.

a. 2-3 heap
b. 1-center problem
c. Circular cylinder
d. 120-cell

52. A _____ is a building where the upper surfaces are triangular and converge on one point. The base of _____s are usually quadrilateral or trilateral, meaning that a _____ usually has four or five faces. A _____'s design, with the majority of the weight closer to the ground, means that less material higher up on the _____ will be pushing down from above.

a. 120-cell
b. 2-3 heap
c. 1-center problem
d. Pyramid

53. _____ is a three-dimensional geometric shape formed by straight lines through a fixed point vertex to the points of a fixed curve directrix.

a. 1-center problem
b. 120-cell
c. 2-3 heap
d. Right circular cone

54. A _____ of a sphere is a circle that runs along the surface of that sphere so as to cut it into two equal halves. The _____ therefore has both the same circumference and the same center as the sphere. It is the largest circle that can be drawn on a given sphere.

a. Cathetus
b. Line segment
c. Perimeter
d. Great circle

55. In computer science an _____ is a data structure consisting of a group of elements that are accessed by indexing. In most programming languages each element has the same data type and the _____ occupies a contiguous area of storage.

Most programming languages have a built-in _____ data type, although what is called an _____ in the language documentation is sometimes really an associative _____.

a. A chemical equation
b. A Mathematical Theory of Communication
c. A posteriori
d. Array

Chapter 14. GEOMETRY USING TRIANGLE CONGRUENCE AND SIMILARITY

1. In mathematics, an _____ or member of a set is any one of the distinct objects that make up that set.

Writing A = {1,2,3,4}, means that the _____s of the set A are the numbers 1, 2, 3 and 4. Groups of _____s of A, for example {1,2}, are subsets of A.

a. Ideal
c. Universal code
b. Order
d. Element

2. _____ In modern English: A problem that severely tests the ability of an inexperienced person.

_____ is the name given to Euclid's fifth proposition in Book 1 of his Elements of geometry, the theorem on isosceles triangles:

Pappus provided the shortest proof of the first part, that if the triangle is ABC with AB being the same length as AC, then comparing it with the triangle ACB will show that two sides and the included angle at A of one are equal to the corresponding parts of the other, so by the fourth proposition the angles at B and C are equal. Euclid's proof was longer and involved the construction of additional triangles.

a. 2-3 heap
c. 120-cell
b. 1-center problem
d. Pons Asinorum

3. In mathematics, the _____ or Pythagoras' theorem is a relation in Euclidean geometry among the three sides of a right triangle. The theorem is named after the Greek mathematician Pythagoras, who by tradition is credited with its discovery and proof, although it is often argued that knowledge of the theory predates him.. The theorem is as follows:

In any right triangle, the area of the square whose side is the hypotenuse is equal to the sum of the areas of the squares whose sides are the two legs.

a. 1-center problem
c. 2-3 heap
b. Pythagorean theorem
d. 120-cell

4. A _____ is one of the basic shapes of geometry: a polygon with three corners or vertices and three sides or edges which are line segments. A _____ with vertices A, B, and C is denoted ABC.

In Euclidean geometry any three non-collinear points determine a unique _____ and a unique plane.

a. Triangle
c. Kepler triangle
b. 1-center problem
d. Fuhrmann circle

5. As an abstract term, _____ means similarity between objects.
a. 2-3 heap
c. 120-cell
b. 1-center problem
d. Congruence

6. In mathematics, a _____ is a statement that can be proved on the basis of explicitly stated or previously agreed assumptions.

Chapter 14. GEOMETRY USING TRIANGLE CONGRUENCE AND SIMILARITY

   a. Logical value
   b. Theorem
   c. Boolean function
   d. Disjunction introduction

7. In game theory, a player's _____ in a game is a complete plan of action for whatever situation might arise; this fully determines the player's behaviour. A player's _____ will determine the action the player will take at any stage of the game, for every possible history of play up to that stage.

A _____ profile is a set of strategies for each player which fully specifies all actions in a game.

   a. Sir Philip Sidney game
   b. Strategy
   c. Correlated equilibrium
   d. Matching pennies

8. In geometry and trigonometry, an _____ is the figure formed by two rays sharing a common endpoint, called the vertex of the _____. The magnitude of the _____ is the 'amount of rotation' that separates the two rays, and can be measured by considering the length of circular arc swept out when one ray is rotated about the vertex to coincide with the other. Where there is no possibility of confusion, the term '_____' is used interchangeably for both the geometric configuration itself and for its angular magnitude.

   a. A chemical equation
   b. A posteriori
   c. A Mathematical Theory of Communication
   d. Angle

9. In geometry, two sets of points are called _____ if one can be transformed into the other by an isometry. Less formally, two figures are _____ if they have the same shape and size, but are in different positions.

In a Euclidean system, congruence is fundamental; it is the counterpart of equality for numbers.

   a. Germ
   b. Gamma test
   c. Function
   d. Congruent

10. _____ are formed when a given transversal line crosses two coplanar lines. The _____ are not necessarily congruent. In the event that the _____ are congruent, these angles can be used to determine the degrees of the other angles of the parallel lines.

   a. Conformal connection
   b. Brocard circle
   c. Corresponding angles
   d. Prismatic pentagonal tiling

11. _____ is a part of mathematics concerned with questions of size, shape, and relative position of figures and with properties of space. _____ is one of the oldest sciences. Initially a body of practical knowledge concerning lengths, areas, and volumes, in the third century BC _____ was put into an axiomatic form by Euclid, whose treatment--Euclidean _____--set a standard for many centuries to follow.

   a. 120-cell
   b. 2-3 heap
   c. Geometry
   d. 1-center problem

12. In geometry, a _____ is a part of a line that is bounded by two distinct end points, and contains every point on the line between its end points. Examples of _____s include the sides of a triangle or square. More generally, when the end points are both vertices of a polygon, the _____ is either an edge if they are adjacent vertices, or otherwise a diagonal.

Chapter 14. GEOMETRY USING TRIANGLE CONGRUENCE AND SIMILARITY 137

a. Transversal line
c. Cuboid

b. Golden angle
d. Line segment

13. _____ is an integrated system of software products provided by _____ Institute that enables the programmer to perform:

- data entry, retrieval, management, and mining
- report writing and graphics
- statistical analysis
- business planning, forecasting, and decision support
- operations research and project management
- quality improvement
- applications development
- data warehousing
- platform independent and remote computing

In addition, _____ has many business solutions that enable large scale software solutions for areas such as IT management, human resource management, financial management, business intelligence, customer relationship management and more.

_____ is driven by _____ programs that define a sequence of operations to be performed on data stored as tables. Although non-programmer graphical user interfaces to _____ exist, most of the time these GUIs are just a front-end to automate or facilitate generation of _____ programs. _____ components expose their functionalities via application programming interfaces, in the form of statements and procedures.

a. Conchoid
c. Blocking

b. FISH
d. SAS

14. In geometry, a _____ is a polygon with four sides or edges and four vertices or corners. Sometimes, the term quadrangle is used, for etymological symmetry with triangle, and sometimes tetragon for consistency with pentagon, hexagon and so on. The interior angles of a _____ add up to 360 degrees of arc.

a. 1-center problem
c. Quadrilateral

b. 120-cell
d. 2-3 heap

15. In mathematics, the _____ of a number n is the number that, when added to n, yields zero. The _____ of n is denoted −n. For example, 7 is −7, because 7 + (−7) = 0, and the _____ of −0.3 is 0.3, because −0.3 + 0.3 = 0.

a. Arity
c. Associativity

b. Additive inverse
d. Algebraic structure

16. In geometry, a _____ is a quadrilateral with two sets of parallel sides. The opposite sides of a _____ are of equal length, and the opposite angles of a _____ are congruent. The three-dimensional counterpart of a _____ is a parallelepiped.

a. 2-3 heap
c. 1-center problem

b. 120-cell
d. Parallelogram

Chapter 14. GEOMETRY USING TRIANGLE CONGRUENCE AND SIMILARITY

17. In geometry, an _____ divides an angle into two equal angles. Each point of an _____ is equidistant from the sides of the angle.
    a. Angle bisector
    c. Interior angle
    b. Inscribed sphere
    d. Exterior angle

18. An angle smaller than a right angle is called an _____ (less than 90 degrees).
    a. Ultraparallel theorem
    c. Integral geometry
    b. Euclidean geometry
    d. Acute angle

19. _____ is the measurement of vertical distance, but has two meanings in common use. It can either indicate how 'tall' something is, or how 'high up' it is. For example one could say 'That is a tall building', or 'That airplane is high up in the sky'.
    a. 120-cell
    c. 2-3 heap
    b. 1-center problem
    d. Height

20. The framework of quantum mechanics requires a careful definition of _____, and a thorough discussion of its practical and philosophical implications.

    _____ is viewed in different ways in the many interpretations of quantum mechanics; however, despite the considerable philosophical differences, they almost universally agree on the practical question of what results from a routine quantum-physics laboratory _____. To describe this, a simple framework to use is the Copenhagen interpretation, and it will be implicitly used in this section; the utility of this approach has been verified countless times, and all other interpretations are necessarily constructed so as to give the same quantitative predictions as this in almost every case.

    a. 1-center problem
    c. Measurement
    b. Dynamic range
    d. Fundamental units

21. In set theory, a _____ is a partially ordered set such that for each t ∈ T, the set {s ∈ T : s < t} is well-ordered by the relation <. For each t ∈ T, the order type of {s ∈ T : s < t} is called the height of t. The height of T itself is the least ordinal greater than the height of each element of T.
    a. Transitive reduction
    c. Definable numbers
    b. Set-theoretic topology
    d. Tree

22. A _____ is generally 'a rough or fragmented geometric shape that can be split into parts, each of which is a reduced-size copy of the whole,' a property called self-similarity. The term was coined by Benoît Mandelbrot in 1975 and was derived from the Latin fractus meaning 'broken' or 'fractured.' A mathematical _____ is based on an equation that undergoes iteration, a form of feedback based on recursion.

Chapter 14. GEOMETRY USING TRIANGLE CONGRUENCE AND SIMILARITY

A _____ often has the following features:

- It has a fine structure at arbitrarily small scales.
- It is too irregular to be easily described in traditional Euclidean geometric language.
- It is self-similar.
- It has a Hausdorff dimension which is greater than its topological dimension.
- It has a simple and recursive definition.

Because they appear similar at all levels of magnification, _____s are often considered to be infinitely complex. Natural objects that approximate _____s to a degree include clouds, mountain ranges, lightning bolts, coastlines, and snow flakes.

a. Logical disjunction
c. Fractal
b. Cube
d. Zero-point energy

23. The _____ is a mathematical curve and one of the earliest fractal curves to have been described. It appeared in a 1904 paper titled 'On a continuous curve without tangents, constructible from elementary geometry' by the Swedish mathematician Helge von Koch. The lesser known _____ is the same as the snowflake, except it starts with a line segment instead of an equilateral triangle.

a. Continuous linear extension
c. Control flow graph
b. Biscuspid
d. Koch curve

24. In mathematics, a self-similar object is exactly or approximately similar to a part of itself. Many objects in the real world, such as coastlines, are statistically self-similar: parts of them show the same statistical properties at many scales. _____ is a typical property of fractals.

a. Gravity set
c. Hausdorff dimension
b. Cantor function
d. Self-similarity

25. In mathematics, the concept of a _____ tries to capture the intuitive idea of a geometrical one-dimensional and continuous object. A simple example is the circle. In everyday use of the term '_____', a straight line is not curved, but in mathematical parlance _____s include straight lines and line segments.

a. Quadrifolium
c. Curve
b. Kappa curve
d. Negative pedal curve

26. A _____, magnetic _____ or mariner's _____ is a navigational instrument for determining direction relative to the earth's magnetic poles. It consists of a magnetized pointer (usually marked on the North end) free to align itself with Earth's magnetic field. The face of the _____ generally highlights the cardinal points of north, south, east and west.

a. Torquetum
c. 1-center problem
b. 120-cell
d. Compass

27. A _____ is a tool with an accurately straight edge used for drawing or cutting straight lines, or checking the straightness of lines. If it has equally spaced markings along its length it is usually called a ruler.

True straightness can in some cases be checked by using a laser line level as an optical _____: it can illuminate an accurately straight line on a flat surface such as the edge of a plank or shelf.

Chapter 14. GEOMETRY USING TRIANGLE CONGRUENCE AND SIMILARITY

a. 2-3 heap
b. Straightedge
c. 1-center problem
d. 120-cell

28. _____ or ruler-and-compass construction is the construction of lengths or angles using only an idealized ruler and compass. Trisecting a segment with ruler and compass.

The ruler to be used is assumed to be infinite in length, has no markings on it and only one edge, and is known as a straightedge. The compass is assumed to collapse when lifted from the page, so may not be directly used to transfer distances.

a. Convergence of measures
b. Convergence of random variables
c. Beth numbers
d. Compass-and-straightedge

29. _____ is the likelihood or chance that something is the case or will happen. Theoretical _____ is used extensively in areas such as statistics, mathematics, science and philosophy to draw conclusions about the likelihood of potential events and the underlying mechanics of complex systems.

The word _____ does not have a consistent direct definition.

a. Discrete random variable
b. Statistical significance
c. Standardized moment
d. Probability

30. A _____ of a curve is the envelope of a family of congruent circles centered on the curve. It generalises the concept of _____ lines.

It is sometimes called the offset curve but the term 'offset' often refers also to translation.

a. Bifolium
b. Cissoid
c. Cycloid
d. Parallel

31. In geometry, an _____ of a triangle is a straight line through a vertex and perpendicular to the opposite side or an extension of the opposite side. The intersection between the side and the _____ is called the foot of the _____. This opposite side is called the base of the _____.

a. Isotomic conjugate
b. A chemical equation
c. A Mathematical Theory of Communication
d. Altitude

32. A _____ is a simple shape of Euclidean geometry consisting of those points in a plane which are at a constant distance, called the radius, from a fixed point, called the center. A _____ with center A is sometimes denoted by the symbol A.

A chord of a _____ is a line segment whose two endpoints lie on the _____.

a. Malfatti circles
b. Circumcircle
c. Circular segment
d. Circle

Chapter 14. GEOMETRY USING TRIANGLE CONGRUENCE AND SIMILARITY   141

33. In geometry, the _____ or circumcircle of a polygon is a circle which passes through all the vertices of the polygon. The center of this circle is called the circumcenter.

A polygon which has a _____ is called a cyclic polygon.

   a. Circular sector
   c. Circumcenter

   b. Circumscribed circle
   d. Tangent lines to circles

34. In geometry, an _____ planar shape or solid is one that is enclosed by and 'fits snugly' inside another geometric shape or solid. Specifically, there must be no object similar to the _____ object but larger and also enclosed by the outer figure.

Familiar examples include circles _____ in polygons, and triangles or regular polygons _____ in circles.

   a. Isometry group
   c. Equiangular polygon

   b. Omnitruncated 5-cell
   d. Inscribed

35. In geometry, the incircle or _____ of a triangle is the largest circle contained in the triangle; it touches the three sides. The center of the incircle is called the triangle's incenter.

An excircle or escribed circle of the triangle is a circle lying outside the triangle, tangent to one of its sides and tangent to the extensions of the other two.

   a. Osculating circle
   c. Incircle

   b. Excircle
   d. Inscribed circle

36. In mathematics, _____ and undefined are used to explain whether or not expressions have meaningful, sensible, and unambiguous values. Not all branches of mathematics come to the same conclusion.

The following expressions are undefined in all contexts, but remarks in the analysis section may apply.

   a. Plugging in
   c. Toy model

   b. LHS
   d. Defined

Chapter 14. GEOMETRY USING TRIANGLE CONGRUENCE AND SIMILARITY

37. The term _____ or centre is used in various contexts in abstract algebra to denote the set of all those elements that commute with all other elements. More specifically:

- The _____ of a group G consists of all those elements x in G such that xg = gx for all g in G. This is a normal subgroup of G.
- The _____ of a ring R is the subset of R consisting of all those elements x of R such that xr = rx for all r in R. The _____ is a commutative subring of R, so R is an algebra over its _____.
- The _____ of an algebra A consists of all those elements x of A such that xa = ax for all a in A. See also: central simple algebra.
- The _____ of a Lie algebra L consists of all those elements x in L such that [x,a] = 0 for all a in L. This is an ideal of the Lie algebra L.
- The _____ of a monoidal category C consists of pairs *a natural isomorphism satisfying certain axioms.*

a. Disk
b. Brute Force
c. Block size
d. Center

38. In geometry, the circumscribed circle or circumcircle of a polygon is a circle which passes through all the vertices of the polygon. The center of this circle is called the _____.

A polygon which has a circumscribed circle is called a cyclic polygon.

a. Circumcenter
b. Circular sector
c. Circumcircle
d. Villarceau circles

39. In trigonometry, the _____ is a function defined as tan x = $^{\sin x}/_{\cos x}$. The function is so-named because it can be defined as the length of a certain segment of a _____ (in the geometric sense) to the unit circle. In plane geometry, a line is _____ to a curve, at some point, if both line and curve pass through the point with the same direction.

a. Tangent
b. Conformal geometry
c. Projective connection
d. Hopf conjectures

40. In geometry, the _____, geometric center, or barycenter of a plane figure X is the intersection of all straight lines that divide X into two parts of equal moment about the line. Informally, it is the 'average' of all points of X. The definition extends to any object X in n-dimensional space: its _____ is the intersection of all hyperplanes that divide X into two parts of equal moment about the hyperplane.

a. 120-cell
b. Line element
c. 1-center problem
d. Centroid

41. In geometry, the _____ to a curve at a given point is the straight line that 'just touches' the curve at that point. As it passes through the point of tangency, the _____ is 'going in the same direction' as the curve, and in this sense it is the best straight-line approximation to the curve at that point. The same definition applies to space curves and curves in n-dimensional Euclidean space.

a. Darboux frame
b. Four-vertex theorem
c. Tangent Line
d. Chern-Weil theory

Chapter 14. GEOMETRY USING TRIANGLE CONGRUENCE AND SIMILARITY

42. In geometry, the circumscribed circle or _____ of a polygon is a circle which passes through all the vertices of the polygon. The center of this circle is called the circumcenter.

A polygon which has a circumscribed circle is called a cyclic polygon.

   a. Circumscribed circle
   b. Five circles theorem
   c. Circumcircle
   d. Circular segment

43. A quadratic equation with real solutions, called roots, which may be real or complex, is given by the _____ : $x = \frac{-b \pm \sqrt{b^2 - 4ac}}{2a}$.

   a. Differential Algebra
   b. Parametric continuity
   c. Quadratic formula
   d. Quotient

44. In mathematics and in the sciences, a _____ (plural: _____e, formulæ or _____s) is a concise way of expressing information symbolically (as in a mathematical or chemical _____), or a general relationship between quantities. One of many famous _____e is Albert Einstein's $E = mc^2$ (see special relativity

In mathematics, a _____ is a key to solve an equation with variables. For example, the problem of determining the volume of a sphere is one that requires a significant amount of integral calculus to solve.

   a. 120-cell
   b. Formula
   c. 2-3 heap
   d. 1-center problem

45. A _____ is a polygon which is equiangular and equilateral. _____s may be convex or star.

These properties apply to both convex and star _____s.

   a. Constructible polygon
   b. Regular decagon
   c. Regular polygon
   d. Star-shaped polygon

46. _____ is a quantity expressing the two-dimensional size of a defined part of a surface, typically a region bounded by a closed curve. The term surface _____ refers to the total _____ of the exposed surface of a 3-dimensional solid, such as the sum of the _____s of the exposed sides of a polyhedron. _____ is an important invariant in the differential geometry of surfaces.

   a. A Mathematical Theory of Communication
   b. Area
   c. A posteriori
   d. A chemical equation

47. In geometry, an _____ is a triangle in which all three sides have equal lengths. In traditional or Euclidean geometry, _____s are also equiangular; that is, all three internal angles are also equal to each other and are each 60°. They are regular polygons, and can therefore also be referred to as regular triangles.

   a. A Mathematical Theory of Communication
   b. Isotomic conjugate
   c. A chemical equation
   d. Equilateral triangle

48. In geometry a _____ is traditionally a plane figure that is bounded by a closed path or circuit, composed of a finite sequence of straight line segments. These segments are called its edges or sides, and the points where two edges meet are the _____'s vertices or corners. The interior of the _____ is sometimes called its body.

a. Parallelogon
b. Polygonal curve
c. Polygon
d. Regular polygon

49. _____ are used in computer graphics to compose images that are three-dimensional in appearance. Usually triangular, _____ arise when an object's surface is modeled, vertices are selected, and the object is rendered in a wire frame model. This is quicker to display than a shaded model; thus the _____ are a stage in computer animation.

a. Visibility polygon
b. Heptadecagon
c. Triskaidecagon
d. Polygons

50. In mathematics, a _____ is a natural number which has exactly two distinct natural number divisors: 1 and itself. An infinitude of _____s exists, as demonstrated by Euclid around 300 BC. The first twenty-five _____s are:

2, 3, 5, 7, 11, 13, 17, 19, 23, 29, 31, 37, 41, 43, 47, 53, 59, 61, 67, 71, 73, 79, 83, 89, 97.

a. Highly composite number
b. Perrin number
c. Pronic number
d. Prime number

51. The _____, in mathematics, is a type of mean or average, which indicates the central tendency or typical value of a set of numbers. It is similar to the arithmetic mean, which is what most people think of with the word 'average,' except that instead of adding the set of numbers and then dividing the sum by the count of numbers in the set, n, the numbers are multiplied and then the nth root of the resulting product is taken.

For instance, the _____ of two numbers, say 2 and 8, is just the square root (i.e., the second root) of their product, 16, which is 4.

a. Stratified sampling
b. Geometric mean
c. Skewness
d. Correlation

52. In statistics, _____ has two related meanings:

- the arithmetic _____.
- the expected value of a random variable, which is also called the population _____.

It is sometimes stated that the '_____' _____s average. This is incorrect if '_____' is taken in the specific sense of 'arithmetic _____' as there are different types of averages: the _____, median, and mode. For instance, average house prices almost always use the median value for the average.

For a real-valued random variable X, the _____ is the expectation of X.

a. Probability
b. Proportional hazards model
c. Statistical population
d. Mean

53. In mathematics, two quantities are called _____ if they vary in such a way that one of the quantities is a constant multiple of the other, or equivalently if they have a constant ratio.

a. 120-cell
b. 1-center problem
c. 2-3 heap
d. Proportional

54. A _____ or a trapezium is a quadrilateral that has at least one pair of parallel lines for sides.

Some authors define it as a quadrilateral having exactly one pair of parallel sides, so as to exclude parallelograms, which otherwise would be regarded as a special type of _____, but most mathematicians use the inclusive definition.

In North America, the term trapezium is used to refer to a quadrilateral with no parallel sides.

a. Trapezium
b. Lozenge
c. Trapezoid
d. Rhomboid

Chapter 15. GEOMETRY USING COORDINATES

1. _____ is the study of geometry using the principles of algebra. That the algebra of the real numbers can be employed to yield results about the linear continuum of geometry relies on the Cantor-Dedekind axiom. Usually the Cartesian coordinate system is applied to manipulate equations for planes, straight lines, and squares, often in two and sometimes in three dimensions of measurement.

   a. Angular eccentricity
   b. Axis-aligned object
   c. Ambient space
   d. Analytic geometry

2. _____ is a part of mathematics concerned with questions of size, shape, and relative position of figures and with properties of space. _____ is one of the oldest sciences. Initially a body of practical knowledge concerning lengths, areas, and volumes, in the third century BC _____ was put into an axiomatic form by Euclid, whose treatment--Euclidean _____--set a standard for many centuries to follow.

   a. 120-cell
   b. 1-center problem
   c. 2-3 heap
   d. Geometry

3. A _____ is one of the basic shapes of geometry: a polygon with three corners or vertices and three sides or edges which are line segments. A _____ with vertices A, B, and C is denoted ABC.

In Euclidean geometry any three non-collinear points determine a unique _____ and a unique plane.

   a. Fuhrmann circle
   b. Kepler triangle
   c. Triangle
   d. 1-center problem

4. In game theory, a player's _____ in a game is a complete plan of action for whatever situation might arise; this fully determines the player's behaviour. A player's _____ will determine the action the player will take at any stage of the game, for every possible history of play up to that stage.

A _____ profile is a set of strategies for each player which fully specifies all actions in a game.

   a. Correlated equilibrium
   b. Sir Philip Sidney game
   c. Matching pennies
   d. Strategy

5. In mathematics and in the sciences, a _____ (plural: _____e, formulæ or _____s) is a concise way of expressing information symbolically (as in a mathematical or chemical _____), or a general relationship between quantities. One of many famous _____e is Albert Einstein's $E = mc^2$ (see special relativity).

In mathematics, a _____ is a key to solve an equation with variables. For example, the problem of determining the volume of a sphere is one that requires a significant amount of integral calculus to solve.

   a. Formula
   b. 2-3 heap
   c. 120-cell
   d. 1-center problem

6. In mathematics, a _____ is, informally, an infinitely vast and infinitely thin sheet. _____s may be thought of as objects in some higher dimensional space, or they may be considered without any outside space, as in the setting of Euclidean geometry

   a. Blocking
   b. Bandwidth
   c. Group
   d. Plane

Chapter 15. GEOMETRY USING COORDINATES

7. _____ is used to describe the steepness, incline, gradient, or grade of a straight line. A higher _____ value indicates a steeper incline. The _____ is defined as the ratio of the 'rise' divided by the 'run' between two points on a line, or in other words, the ratio of the altitude change to the horizontal distance between any two points on the line.
    a. Slope
    b. Number line
    c. Point plotting
    d. Cognitively Guided Instruction

8. A _____ is a mathematical manipulative often used to explore basic concepts in plane geometry such as perimeter, area or the characteristics of triangles and other polygons. Consisting of a physical board with a certain number of nails half driven in, in a symmetrical square five-by-five array, students are encouraged to place rubber bands around the pegs to model various geometric concepts or to solve other mathematical puzzles. Two-dimensional representations of the _____ may be applied to ordinary paper using rubber stamps or special '_____ paper' with diagrams of _____s may be used to help capture a student's explanations of the concept they have discovered or illustrated on the _____.
    a. Cuisenaire rods
    b. Van Hiele levels
    c. 1-center problem
    d. Geoboard

9. In geometry, a _____ is a part of a line that is bounded by two distinct end points, and contains every point on the line between its end points. Examples of _____s include the sides of a triangle or square. More generally, when the end points are both vertices of a polygon, the _____ is either an edge if they are adjacent vertices, or otherwise a diagonal.
    a. Golden angle
    b. Transversal line
    c. Cuboid
    d. Line segment

10. In mathematics, the _____ is an approach to finding a particular solution to certain inhomogeneous ordinary differential equations and recurrence relations. It is closely related to the annihilator method, but instead of using a particular kind of differential operator in order to find the best possible form of the particular solution, a 'guess' is made as to the appropriate form, which is then tested by differentiating the resulting equation. In this sense, the _____ is less formal but more intuitive than the annihilator method.
    a. Linear differential equation
    b. Differential algebraic equations
    c. Method of undetermined coefficients
    d. Phase line

11. A _____ of a curve is the envelope of a family of congruent circles centered on the curve. It generalises the concept of _____ lines.

It is sometimes called the offset curve but the term 'offset' often refers also to translation.

    a. Cissoid
    b. Bifolium
    c. Cycloid
    d. Parallel

12. The existence and properties of _____ are the basis of Euclid's parallel postulate. _____ are two lines on the same plane that do not intersect even assuming that lines extend to infinity in either direction.
    a. Parallel lines
    b. Square wheel
    c. Spidron
    d. Vertical translation

13. In mathematics, a _____ is a natural number which has exactly two distinct natural number divisors: 1 and itself. An infinitude of _____s exists, as demonstrated by Euclid around 300 BC. The first twenty-five _____s are:

Chapter 15. GEOMETRY USING COORDINATES

2, 3, 5, 7, 11, 13, 17, 19, 23, 29, 31, 37, 41, 43, 47, 53, 59, 61, 67, 71, 73, 79, 83, 89, 97.

a. Pronic number
b. Highly composite number
c. Perrin number
d. Prime number

14. A _____ is a simple shape of Euclidean geometry consisting of those points in a plane which are at a constant distance, called the radius, from a fixed point, called the center. A _____ with center A is sometimes denoted by the symbol A.

A chord of a _____ is a line segment whose two endpoints lie on the _____.

a. Malfatti circles
b. Circumcircle
c. Circular segment
d. Circle

15. In mathematics, the concept of a '_____' is used to describe the behavior of a function as its argument or input either 'gets close' to some point, or as the argument becomes arbitrarily large; or the behavior of a sequence's elements as their index increases indefinitely. _____s are used in calculus and other branches of mathematical analysis to define derivatives and continuity.

In formulas, _____ is usually abbreviated as lim.

a. Copula
b. Duality
c. Contact
d. Limit

16. In mathematics, the _____ system is a two-dimensional coordinate system in which each point on a plane is determined by an angle and a distance. The _____ system is especially useful in situations where the relationship between two points is most easily expressed in terms of angles and distance; in the more familiar Cartesian or rectangular coordinate system, such a relationship can only be found through trigonometric formulation.

As the coordinate system is two-dimensional, each point is determined by two _____s: the radial coordinate and the angular coordinate.

a. Sequence alignment
b. Polar coordinate
c. Vampire
d. Sir Isaac Newton

17. In mathematics an _____ , a 'falling short') is a conic section, the locus of points in a plane such that the sum of the distances to two fixed points is equal to a given constant. The two fixed points are then called foci.

Another way is to define it as the path traced out by a point whose distance from a focus maintains a constant ratio less than one with its distance from a straight line not passing through the focus, called the directrix.

a. A chemical equation
b. A Mathematical Theory of Communication
c. A posteriori
d. Ellipse

Chapter 15. GEOMETRY USING COORDINATES

18. In mathematics, the _____ is a conic section, the intersection of a right circular conical surface and a plane parallel to a generating straight line of that surface. Given a point and a line that lie in a plane, the locus of points in that plane that are equidistant to them is a _____.

A particular case arises when the plane is tangent to the conical surface of a circle.

a. Parabola
c. Directrix

b. Dandelin sphere
d. Matrix representation of conic sections

19. The term _____ or centre is used in various contexts in abstract algebra to denote the set of all those elements that commute with all other elements. More specifically:

- The _____ of a group G consists of all those elements x in G such that xg = gx for all g in G. This is a normal subgroup of G.
- The _____ of a ring R is the subset of R consisting of all those elements x of R such that xr = rx for all r in R. The _____ is a commutative subring of R, so R is an algebra over its _____.
- The _____ of an algebra A consists of all those elements x of A such that xa = ax for all a in A. See also: central simple algebra.
- The _____ of a Lie algebra L consists of all those elements x in L such that [x,a] = 0 for all a in L. This is an ideal of the Lie algebra L.
- The _____ of a monoidal category C consists of pairs *a natural isomorphism satisfying certain axioms*.

a. Center
c. Disk

b. Block size
d. Brute Force

20. In geometry, the _____, geometric center, or barycenter of a plane figure X is the intersection of all straight lines that divide X into two parts of equal moment about the line. Informally, it is the 'average' of all points of X. The definition extends to any object X in n-dimensional space: its _____ is the intersection of all hyperplanes that divide X into two parts of equal moment about the hyperplane.

a. 1-center problem
c. Line element

b. 120-cell
d. Centroid

21. In geometry and trigonometry, an _____ is the figure formed by two rays sharing a common endpoint, called the vertex of the _____. The magnitude of the _____ is the 'amount of rotation' that separates the two rays, and can be measured by considering the length of circular arc swept out when one ray is rotated about the vertex to coincide with the other. Where there is no possibility of confusion, the term '_____' is used interchangeably for both the geometric configuration itself and for its angular magnitude.

a. Angle
c. A chemical equation

b. A posteriori
d. A Mathematical Theory of Communication

22. In geometry, the _____ is a circle that can be constructed for any given triangle. It is so named because it passes through nine significant points, six lying on the triangle itself. They include:

- The midpoint of each side of the triangle
- The foot of each altitude
- The midpoint of the segment of each altitude from its vertex to the orthocenter

The _____ is also known as Feuerbach's circle, Euler's circle, Terquem's circle, the six-points circle, the twelve-points circle, the n-point circle, the medioscribed circle, the mid circle or the circum-midcircle.

Figure 1

The diagram above shows the nine significant points of the _____.

   a. Circumscribed circle   b. Nine-point circle
   c. Circular sector   d. Malfatti circles

23. In mathematics, a _____ is a statement that can be proved on the basis of explicitly stated or previously agreed assumptions.

   a. Disjunction introduction   b. Boolean function
   c. Theorem   d. Logical value

Chapter 16. GEOMETRY USING TRANSFORMATIONS

1. _____ was the Allied codename for any of several German teleprinter stream ciphers used during World War II. Enciphered teleprinter traffic was used between German High Command and Army Group commanders in the field, so its intelligence value was of the highest strategic value to the Allies. This traffic normally passed over landlines, but as German forces extended their reach out of western Europe, they had to resort to wireless transmission.
   - a. Function
   - b. Divide and conquer
   - c. Colossus
   - d. Fish

2. _____ is a part of mathematics concerned with questions of size, shape, and relative position of figures and with properties of space. _____ is one of the oldest sciences. Initially a body of practical knowledge concerning lengths, areas, and volumes, in the third century BC _____ was put into an axiomatic form by Euclid, whose treatment--Euclidean _____--set a standard for many centuries to follow.
   - a. 2-3 heap
   - b. 120-cell
   - c. 1-center problem
   - d. Geometry

3. A _____ is one of the basic shapes of geometry: a polygon with three corners or vertices and three sides or edges which are line segments. A _____ with vertices A, B, and C is denoted ABC.

In Euclidean geometry any three non-collinear points determine a unique _____ and a unique plane.

   - a. 1-center problem
   - b. Triangle
   - c. Kepler triangle
   - d. Fuhrmann circle

4. _____ generally conveys two primary meanings. The first is an imprecise sense of harmonious or aesthetically-pleasing proportionality and balance; such that it reflects beauty or perfection. The second meaning is a precise and well-defined concept of balance or 'patterned self-similarity' that can be demonstrated or proved according to the rules of a formal system: by geometry, through physics or otherwise.
   - a. Tessellation
   - b. Symmetry breaking
   - c. Symmetry
   - d. Molecular symmetry

5. In game theory, a player's _____ in a game is a complete plan of action for whatever situation might arise; this fully determines the player's behaviour. A player's _____ will determine the action the player will take at any stage of the game, for every possible history of play up to that stage.

A _____ profile is a set of strategies for each player which fully specifies all actions in a game.

   - a. Sir Philip Sidney game
   - b. Correlated equilibrium
   - c. Strategy
   - d. Matching pennies

6. An _____ is an artifact, usually two-dimensional (a picture), that has a similar appearance to some subject--usually a physical object or a person.

_____s may be two-dimensional, such as a photograph, screen display, and as well as a three-dimensional, such as a statue. They may be captured by optical devices--such as cameras, mirrors, lenses, telescopes, microscopes, etc.

Chapter 16. GEOMETRY USING TRANSFORMATIONS

a. A chemical equation
b. A posteriori
c. A Mathematical Theory of Communication
d. Image

7. _____ is the interpreting of the meaning of a text and the subsequent production of an equivalent text, likewise called a '_____,' that communicates the same message in another language. The text to be translated is called the 'source text,' and the language that it is to be translated into is called the 'target language'; the final product is sometimes called the 'target text.'

_____ must take into account constraints that include context, the rules of grammar of the two languages, their writing conventions, and their idioms. A common misconception is that there exists a simple word-for-word correspondence between any two languages, and that _____ is a straightforward mechanical process; such a word-for-word _____, however, cannot take into account context, grammar, conventions, and idioms.

a. 1-center problem
b. 120-cell
c. 2-3 heap
d. Translation

8. In mathematics, _____ and undefined are used to explain whether or not expressions have meaningful, sensible, and unambiguous values. Not all branches of mathematics come to the same conclusion.

The following expressions are undefined in all contexts, but remarks in the analysis section may apply.

a. LHS
b. Defined
c. Toy model
d. Plugging in

9. In mathematics, an _____, isometric isomorphism or congruence mapping is a distance-preserving isomorphism between metric spaces. Geometric figures which can be related by an _____ are called congruent.

Isometries are often used in constructions where one space is embedded in another space.

a. A Mathematical Theory of Communication
b. Unary function
c. A chemical equation
d. Isometry

10. In the study of metric spaces in mathematics, there are various notions of two metrics on the same underlying space being 'the same', or _____.

In the following, M will denote a non-empty set and d_1 and d_2 will denote two metrics on M.

The two metrics d_1 and d_2 are said to be topologically _____ if they generate the same topology on M.

a. A posteriori
b. A Mathematical Theory of Communication
c. A chemical equation
d. Equivalent

11. In geometry, a _____ is a part of a line that is bounded by two distinct end points, and contains every point on the line between its end points. Examples of _____s include the sides of a triangle or square. More generally, when the end points are both vertices of a polygon, the _____ is either an edge if they are adjacent vertices, or otherwise a diagonal.

Chapter 16. GEOMETRY USING TRANSFORMATIONS

a. Transversal line
b. Cuboid
c. Golden angle
d. Line segment

12. In geometry and trigonometry, an _____ is the figure formed by two rays sharing a common endpoint, called the vertex of the _____. The magnitude of the _____ is the 'amount of rotation' that separates the two rays, and can be measured by considering the length of circular arc swept out when one ray is rotated about the vertex to coincide with the other. Where there is no possibility of confusion, the term '_____' is used interchangeably for both the geometric configuration itself and for its angular magnitude.
   a. A chemical equation
   b. A posteriori
   c. A Mathematical Theory of Communication
   d. Angle

13. A _____ is a movement of an object in a circular motion. A two-dimensional object rotates around a center of _____. A three-dimensional object rotates around a line called an axis.
   a. Rotation
   b. Square lattice
   c. Steiner-Lehmus theorem
   d. Homothetic center

14. The term _____ or centre is used in various contexts in abstract algebra to denote the set of all those elements that commute with all other elements. More specifically:

   - The _____ of a group G consists of all those elements x in G such that xg = gx for all g in G. This is a normal subgroup of G.
   - The _____ of a ring R is the subset of R consisting of all those elements x of R such that xr = rx for all r in R. The _____ is a commutative subring of R, so R is an algebra over its _____.
   - The _____ of an algebra A consists of all those elements x of A such that xa = ax for all a in A. See also: central simple algebra.
   - The _____ of a Lie algebra L consists of all those elements x in L such that [x,a] = 0 for all a in L. This is an ideal of the Lie algebra L.
   - The _____ of a monoidal category C consists of pairs *a natural isomorphism satisfying certain axioms*.

   a. Brute Force
   b. Block size
   c. Center
   d. Disk

15. Initial objects are also called _____, and terminal objects are also called final.
   a. Colimit
   b. Coterminal
   c. Terminal object
   d. Direct limit

16. In geometry, the _____, geometric center, or barycenter of a plane figure X is the intersection of all straight lines that divide X into two parts of equal moment about the line. Informally, it is the 'average' of all points of X. The definition extends to any object X in n-dimensional space: its _____ is the intersection of all hyperplanes that divide X into two parts of equal moment about the hyperplane.
   a. 120-cell
   b. Line element
   c. 1-center problem
   d. Centroid

Chapter 16. GEOMETRY USING TRANSFORMATIONS

17. In mathematics the concept of a _____ generalizes notions such as 'length', 'area', and 'volume'. Informally, given some base set, a '_____' is any consistent assignment of 'sizes' to the subsets of the base set. Depending on the application, the 'size' of a subset may be interpreted as its physical size, the amount of something that lies within the subset, or the probability that some random process will yield a result within the subset.
 a. Cusp
 b. Measure
 c. Lattice
 d. Congruent

18. In geometry, a _____ is a type of isometry of the Euclidean plane: the combination of a reflection in a line and a translation along that line. Reversing the order of combining gives the same result. Depending on context, we may consider a reflection a special case, where the translation vector is the zero vector.
 a. Rotation of axes
 b. Hubbard-Stratonovich transformation
 c. Glide reflection
 d. Surjective

19. _____, line symmetry, mirror symmetry, mirror-image symmetry, or bilateral symmetry is symmetry with respect to reflection.

In 2D there is an axis of symmetry, in 3D a plane of symmetry. An object or figure which is indistinguishable from its transformed image is called mirror symmetric (see mirror image.)

 a. Hypotenuse
 b. Line segment
 c. Circumscribed sphere
 d. Reflection symmetry

20. _____ is the likelihood or chance that something is the case or will happen. Theoretical _____ is used extensively in areas such as statistics, mathematics, science and philosophy to draw conclusions about the likelihood of potential events and the underlying mechanics of complex systems.

The word _____ does not have a consistent direct definition.

 a. Statistical significance
 b. Probability
 c. Standardized moment
 d. Discrete random variable

21. A _____, from the French patron, is a type of theme of recurring events of or objects, sometimes referred to as elements of a set. These elements repeat in a predictable manner. It can be a template or model which can be used to generate things or parts of a thing, especially if the things that are created have enough in common for the underlying _____ to be inferred, in which case the things are said to exhibit the unique _____.
 a. 1-center problem
 b. Pattern
 c. 120-cell
 d. 2-3 heap

22. As an abstract term, _____ means similarity between objects.
 a. 120-cell
 b. 2-3 heap
 c. Congruence
 d. 1-center problem

23. In geometry, two sets of points are called _____ if one can be transformed into the other by an isometry. Less formally, two figures are _____ if they have the same shape and size, but are in different positions.

In a Euclidean system, congruence is fundamental; it is the counterpart of equality for numbers.

| a. Function | b. Germ |
| c. Gamma test | d. Congruent |

24. The _____ of an object located in some space refers to the part of space occupied by the object as determined by its external boundary -- abstracting from other aspects the object may have such as its colour, content as well as from the object's position and orientation in space, and its size.

According to famous mathematician and statistician David George Kendall, _____ may be defined as

Simple two-dimensional _____s can be described by basic geometry such as points, line, curves, plane, and so on. _____s that occur in the physical world are often quite complex; they may be arbitrarily curved as studied by differential geometry as for plants or coastlines.)

| a. Spidron | b. Parallel lines |
| c. Confocal | d. Shape |

25. In geometry a _____ is traditionally a plane figure that is bounded by a closed path or circuit, composed of a finite sequence of straight line segments. These segments are called its edges or sides, and the points where two edges meet are the _____'s vertices or corners. The interior of the _____ is sometimes called its body.

| a. Regular polygon | b. Polygonal curve |
| c. Parallelogon | d. Polygon |

26. _____ are used in computer graphics to compose images that are three-dimensional in appearance. Usually triangular, _____ arise when an object's surface is modeled, vertices are selected, and the object is rendered in a wire frame model. This is quicker to display than a shaded model; thus the _____ are a stage in computer animation.

| a. Visibility polygon | b. Polygons |
| c. Heptadecagon | d. Triskaidecagon |

27. In linear algebra, two n-by-n matrices A and B over the field K are called _____ if there exists an invertible n-by-n matrix P over K such that

$$P^{-1}AP = B.$$

One of the meanings of the term similarity transformation is such a transformation of a matrix A into a matrix B.

Similarity is an equivalence relation on the space of square matrices.

Chapter 16. GEOMETRY USING TRANSFORMATIONS

_____ matrices share many properties:

- rank
- determinant
- trace
- eigenvalues
- characteristic polynomial
- minimal polynomial
- elementary divisors

There are two reasons for these facts:

- two _____ matrices can be thought of as describing the same linear map, but with respect to different bases
- the map $X \mapsto P^{-1}XP$ is an automorphism of the associative algebra of all n-by-n matrices, as the one-object case of the above category of all matrices.

Because of this, for a given matrix A, one is interested in finding a simple 'normal form' B which is _____ to A -- the study of A then reduces to the study of the simpler matrix B.

a. Dense
c. Blinding
b. Coherence
d. Similar

28. In mathematics, _____ is a name for a pedagogic theory for teaching Euclidean geometry, based on the Erlangen programme. Felix Klein, who pioneered this point of view, was himself interested in mathematical education. It took many years, though, for his 'modern' point of view to have much effect, with the synthetic geometry remaining dominant.

a. Complex geometry
c. The Geometry Center
b. Loomis-Whitney inequality
d. Transformation geometry

29. In mathematics, the _____ or Pythagoras' theorem is a relation in Euclidean geometry among the three sides of a right triangle. The theorem is named after the Greek mathematician Pythagoras, who by tradition is credited with its discovery and proof, although it is often argued that knowledge of the theory predates him.. The theorem is as follows:

In any right triangle, the area of the square whose side is the hypotenuse is equal to the sum of the areas of the squares whose sides are the two legs.

a. 2-3 heap
c. 120-cell
b. 1-center problem
d. Pythagorean theorem

30. In mathematics, a _____ is a statement that can be proved on the basis of explicitly stated or previously agreed assumptions.

a. Logical value
c. Boolean function
b. Disjunction introduction
d. Theorem

Chapter 16. GEOMETRY USING TRANSFORMATIONS

31. In computational complexity theory, the complexity class _____ is the union of the classes in the exponential hierarchy.

$$\text{ELEMENTARY} = \text{EXP} \cup \text{2EXP} \cup \text{3EXP} \cup \cdots$$
$$= \text{DTIME}(2^n) \cup \text{DTIME}(2^{2^n}) \cup \text{DTIME}(2^{2^{2^n}}) \cup \cdots$$

The name was coined by Laszlo Kalmar, in the context of recursive functions and undecidability; most problems in it are far from _____. Some natural recursive problems lie outside _____, and are thus NONELEMENTARY.

a. A posteriori
b. Elementary
c. A chemical equation
d. A Mathematical Theory of Communication

32. An _____ is one that cannot be compressed because it lacks sufficient repeating sequences. Whether a string is compressible will often depend on the algorithm being used. Some examples may illuminate this.

a. Arithmetic coding
b. Entropy encoding
c. A Mathematical Theory of Communication
d. Incompressible string

33. _____ is the study of the principles of valid demonstration and inference. _____ is a branch of philosophy, a part of the classical trivium of grammar, _____, and rhetoric. of λογικῐΌες, 'possessed of reason, intellectual, dialectical, argumentative', from λῐΌεγος logos, 'word, thought, idea, argument, account, reason, or principle'.

a. Counterpart theory
b. Satisfiability
c. Logic
d. Boolean function

34. In logic and mathematics, _____ or not is an operation on logical values, for example, the logical value of a proposition, that sends true to false and false to true. Intuitively, the _____ of a proposition holds exactly when that proposition does not hold. In grammar, nor is an adverb which acts as a coordinating conjunction.

a. 1-center problem
b. Negation
c. Syntax
d. Sentence diagram

35. A _____ is a mathematical table used in logic -- specifically in connection with Boolean algebra, boolean functions, and propositional calculus -- to compute the functional values of logical expressions on each of their functional arguments, that is, on each combination of values taken by their logical variables. In particular, _____s can be used to tell whether a propositional expression is true for all legitimate input values, that is, logically valid.

The pattern of reasoning that the _____ tabulates was Frege's, Peirce's, and Schröder's by 1880.

a. 2-3 heap
b. 1-center problem
c. 120-cell
d. Truth table

36. The mathematical concept of a _____ expresses the intuitive idea of deterministic dependence between two quantities, one of which is viewed as primary and the other as secondary. A _____ then is a way to associate a unique output for each input of a specified type, for example, a real number or an element of a given set.

Chapter 16. GEOMETRY USING TRANSFORMATIONS

    a. Function
    b. Going up
    c. Coherent
    d. Grill

37. In logic and mathematics, or, also known as logical _____ or inclusive _____ is a logical operator that results in true whenever one or more of its operands are true. In grammar, or is a coordinating conjunction. In ordinary language 'or' rather has the meaning of exclusive _____.
    a. Zero-point energy
    b. Cube
    c. Triquetra
    d. Disjunction

38. In logic, two sentences (either in a formal language or a natural language) may be joined by means of a _____ to form a compound sentence. The truth-value of the compound is uniquely determined by the truth-values of the simpler sentences. The _____ therefore represents a function, and since the value of the compound sentence is a truth-value, it is called a truth-function and the _____ is called a 'truth-functional connective'.
    a. Logical connective
    b. Satisfiability
    c. Fallacies of definition
    d. Set theory

39. A _____ is a 2D geometric symbolic representation of information according to some visualization technique. Sometimes, the technique uses a 3D visualization which is then projected onto the 2D surface. The word graph is sometimes used as a synonym for _____.
    a. 120-cell
    b. 2-3 heap
    c. 1-center problem
    d. Diagram

40. A hypothesis consists either of a suggested explanation for an observable phenomenon or of a reasoned proposal predicting a possible causal correlation among multiple phenomena. The term derives from the Greek, hypotithenai meaning 'to put under' or 'to suppose.' The scientific method requires that one can test a scientific hypothesis. Scientists generally base such _____ on previous observations or on extensions of scientific theories.
    a. Hypotheses
    b. 120-cell
    c. 2-3 heap
    d. 1-center problem

41. In mathematics, an _____ is a statement about the relative size or order of two objects, or about whether they are the same or not

- The notation a < b means that a is less than b.
- The notation a > b means that a is greater than b.
- The notation a ≠ b means that a is not equal to b, but does not say that one is bigger than the other or even that they can be compared in size.

In all these cases, a is not equal to b, hence, '_____'.

These relations are known as strict _____

- The notation a ≤ b means that a is less than or equal to b;
- The notation a ≥ b means that a is greater than or equal to b;

Chapter 16. GEOMETRY USING TRANSFORMATIONS

An additional use of the notation is to show that one quantity is much greater than another, normally by several orders of magnitude.

- The notation a << b means that a is much less than b.
- The notation a >> b means that a is much greater than b.

If the sense of the _____ is the same for all values of the variables for which its members are defined, then the _____ is called an 'absolute' or 'unconditional' _____. If the sense of an _____ holds only for certain values of the variables involved, but is reversed or destroyed for other values of the variables, it is called a conditional _____.

An _____ may appear unsolvable because it only states whether a number is larger or smaller than another number; but it is possible to apply the same operations for equalities to inequalities. For example, to find x for the _____ 10x > 23 one would divide 23 by 10.

   a. Inequality
   b. A posteriori
   c. A Mathematical Theory of Communication
   d. A chemical equation

42. In propositional logic, contraposition is a logical relationship between two statements of material implication. A proposition Q is materially implicated by a proposition P when the following relationship holds:

$$(P \to Q)$$

In vernacular terms, this states 'If P then Q', or, 'If Socrates is a man then Socrates is human.' In a conditional such as this, P is called the antecedent and Q the consequent. One statement is the _____ of the other just when its antecedent is the negated consequent of the other, and vice-versa.

   a. Contour map
   b. Control chart
   c. Contrapositive
   d. Continuous signal

43. In mathematics, the _____ of a number n is the number that, when added to n, yields zero. The _____ of n is denoted −n. For example, 7 is −7, because 7 + (−7) = 0, and the _____ of −0.3 is 0.3, because −0.3 + 0.3 = 0.
   a. Additive inverse
   b. Arity
   c. Algebraic structure
   d. Associativity

44. _____ is a concept in traditional logic referring to a 'type of immediate inference in which from a given proposition another proposition is inferred which has as its subject the predicate of the original proposition and as its predicate the subject of the original proposition (the quality of the proposition being retained).'
   a. Field
   b. Foci
   c. Boolean algebra
   d. Converse Logic

Chapter 16. GEOMETRY USING TRANSFORMATIONS

45. _____, in logic and fields that rely on it such as mathematics and philosophy, is a biconditional logical connective between statements. In that it is biconditional, the connective can be likened to the standard material conditional ('if') combined with its reverse ('only if'); hence the name. The result is that the truth of either one of the connected statements requires the truth of the other.
   a. Enumerative definition
   b. Algebraic logic
   c. If and only if
   d. Existential graph

46. In propositional logic, a set of Boolean operators is called _____ if it permits the realisation of any possible truth table.

Using a complete Boolean algebra which does not include XOR (such as the well-known AND OR NOT set), this function can be realised as follows:

(a or b) and not (a and b.)

However, other complete Boolean algebras are possible, such as NAND or NOR (either gate can form a complete Boolean algebra by itself - the proof is detailed on their pages.)

   a. First-order predicate calculus
   b. Counterfactual conditional
   c. Logical biconditional
   d. Sufficient

47. In graph theory, an _____ is a path in a graph which visits each edge exactly once. Similarly, an Eulerian circuit is an _____ which starts and ends on the same vertex. They were first discussed by Leonhard Euler while solving the famous Seven Bridges of Königsberg problem in 1736.
   a. Independent set
   b. Adjacent vertex
   c. Eulerian path
   d. Isomorphism of graphs

48. A _____ is a simplified conventional pictorial representation of an electrical circuit. It shows the components of the circuit as simplified standard symbols, and the power and signal connections between the devices. Arrangement of the components interconnections on the diagram does not correspond to their physical locations in the finished device.
   a. 1-center problem
   b. Circuit diagram
   c. 2-3 heap
   d. 120-cell

49. In calculus, the _____ is a formula for the derivative of the composite of two functions.

In intuitive terms, if a variable, y, depends on a second variable, u, which in turn depends on a third variable, x, then the rate of change of y with respect to x can be computed as the rate of change of y with respect to u multiplied by the rate of change of u with respect to x. Schematically,

$$\frac{dy}{dx} = \frac{dy}{du} \cdot \frac{du}{dx}.$$

For an explanation of notation used in this section, see Function composition.

The _____ states that, under appropriate conditions,

$$(f \circ g)'(x) = f'(g(x))g'(x),$$

which in short form is written as

$$(f \circ g)' = f' \circ g \cdot g'.$$

Alternatively, in the Leibniz notation, the _____ is

$$\frac{dy}{dx} = \frac{dy}{du} \cdot \frac{du}{dx}.$$

In integration, the counterpart to the _____ is the substitution rule.

a. Chain rule
c. 120-cell
b. 1-center problem
d. Product rule

50. In cryptography, the _____ was a method devised by Polish mathematician-cryptologist Jerzy Różycki, at the Polish General Staff's Cipher Bureau, to facilitate decrypting German Enigma messages. This method sometimes made it possible to determine which of the Enigma machine's rotors was at the far right, that is, in the position where the rotor always revolved at every depression of a key.

- Biuro Szyfrów

a. Clock
c. Bombe
b. FROSTBURG
d. TWIRL

51. In mathematics, _____ is a system of arithmetic for integers, where numbers 'wrap around' after they reach a certain value -- the modulus. _____ was introduced by Carl Friedrich Gauss in his book Disquisitiones Arithmeticae, published in 1801.

A familiar use of _____ is its use in the 24-hour clock: the arithmetic of time-keeping in which the day runs from midnight to midnight and is divided into 24 hours, numbered from 0 to 23.

a. Multiplicative group of integers modulo n
c. Residue number system
b. Discrete logarithm
d. Modular arithmetic

Chapter 16. GEOMETRY USING TRANSFORMATIONS

52. The word _____ is the Latin ablative of modulus which itself means 'a small measure.' It was introduced into mathematics in the book Disquisitiones Arithmeticae by Carl Friedrich Gauss in 1801. Ever since, however, '_____' has gained many meanings, some exact and some imprecise.

- (This usage is from Gauss's book.) Given the integers a, b and n, the expression a ≡ b (mod n) means that a − b is a multiple of n, or equivalently, a and b both leave the same remainder when divided by n. For more details, see modular arithmetic.

- In computing, given two numbers (either integer or real), a and n, a _____ n is the remainder after numerical division of a by n, under certain constraints. See _____ operation.

   a. Modulo
   c. Per mil
   b. Predictor-corrector method
   d. Quotition

53. In mathematics and computer science, _____ is the study of graphs: mathematical structures used to model pairwise relations between objects from a certain collection. A 'graph' in this context refers to a collection of vertices or 'nodes' and a collection of edges that connect pairs of vertices. A graph may be undirected, meaning that there is no distinction between the two vertices associated with each edge, or its edges may be directed from one vertex to another; see graph for more detailed definitions and for other variations in the types of graphs that are commonly considered.

   a. Partial equivalence relation
   c. Discrete mathematics
   b. Graph theory
   d. Pooling design

54. In graph theory, a _____ is a digraph with weighted edges. These _____s have become an especially useful concept in analysing the interaction between biology and mathematics. Using _____s of all types; various applications based on the creativity of the mathematician along with their environment can be evaluated in all sorts of manners.

   a. Chord
   c. Colossus
   b. Copula
   d. Network

55. In geometry, a _____ is a special kind of point, usually a corner of a polygon, polyhedron, or higher dimensional polytope. In the geometry of curves a _____ is a point of where the first derivative of curvature is zero. In graph theory, a _____ is the fundamental unit out of which graphs are formed

   a. Duality
   c. Dini
   b. Crib
   d. Vertex

56. A _____ is a structure built to span a gorge, valley, road, railroad track, river, body of water for the purpose of providing passage over the obstacle. Designs of _____s will vary depending on the function of the _____ and the nature of the terrain where the _____ is to be constructed. Roman _____ of Córdoba, Spain, built in the 1st century BC. Ponte di Pietra in Verona, Italy. A log _____ in the French Alps near Vallorcine. An English 18th century example of a _____ in the Palladian style, with shops on the span: Pulteney _____, Bath A Han Dynasty Chinese miniature model of two residential towers joined by a _____

The first _____s were made by nature -- as simple as a log fallen across a stream.

Chapter 16. GEOMETRY USING TRANSFORMATIONS

a. 2-3 heap
c. 1-center problem
b. Bridge
d. 120-cell

57. The word _____ has many distinct meanings in different fields of knowledge, depending on their methodologies and the context of discussion. Broadly speaking we can say that a _____ is some kind of belief or claim that (supposedly) explains, asserts, or consolidates some class of claims. Additionally, in contrast with a theorem the statement of the _____ is generally accepted only in some tentative fashion as opposed to regarding it as having been conclusively established.
   a. Per mil
   c. Defined
   b. Transport of structure
   d. Theory

58. _____ is an adjective meaning contiguous, adjoining or abutting.

In geometry, _____ is when sides meet to make an angle.

In trigonometry the _____ side of a right angled triangle is the cathetus next to the angle in question.

   a. Affine geometry
   c. Ambient space
   b. Ordered geometry
   d. Adjacent

59. In geometry, _____ are angles that have a common ray coming out of the vertex going between two other rays. In other words, they are angles that are side by side, or adjacent.

An angle with a ray connected to a common point down the center.

   a. A Mathematical Theory of Communication
   c. Elliptic geometry
   b. Adjacent angles
   d. Erlangen Program

60. In graph theory, a _____ in a graph is a sequence of vertices such that from each of its vertices there is an edge to the next vertex in the sequence. The first vertex is called the start vertex and the last vertex is called the end vertex. Both of them are called end or terminal vertices of the _____.
   a. Blinding
   c. Path
   b. Deltoid
   d. Class

61. In graph theory, a _____ is a graph which can be embedded in the plane.

A nonplanar graph is the one which cannot be drawn in the plane without edge intersections.

A _____ already drawn in the plane without edge intersections is called a plane graph or planar embedding of the graph.

   a. Dense graph
   c. Sparse graph
   b. Vertex-transitive graph
   d. Planar graph

Chapter 16. GEOMETRY USING TRANSFORMATIONS

62. In mathematics and in the sciences, a _____ (plural: _____e, formulæ or _____s) is a concise way of expressing information symbolically (as in a mathematical or chemical _____), or a general relationship between quantities. One of many famous _____e is Albert Einstein's E = mc² (see special relativity

In mathematics, a _____ is a key to solve an equation with variables. For example, the problem of determining the volume of a sphere is one that requires a significant amount of integral calculus to solve.

- a. 120-cell
- b. Formula
- c. 2-3 heap
- d. 1-center problem

63. A _____ is often defined as a geometric object with flat faces and straight edges.

This definition of a _____ is not very precise, and to a modern mathematician is quite unsatisfactory. Grünbaum observed that:

The Original Sin in the theory of polyhedra goes back to Euclid, and through Kepler, Poinsot, Cauchy and many others ...

- a. Polyhedron
- b. 120-cell
- c. 2-3 heap
- d. 1-center problem

64. The _____ in operations research is a problem in discrete or combinatorial optimization. It is a prominent illustration of a class of problems in computational complexity theory which are classified as NP-hard.

The problem is: given a number of cities and the costs of travelling from any city to any other city, what is the least-cost round-trip route that visits each city exactly once and then returns to the starting city?

Given a number of cities and the costs of travelling from any city to any other city, what is the least-cost round-trip route that visits each city exactly once and then returns to the starting city?

The size of the solution space is!/2 for n > 2, where n is the number of cities.

- a. New digraph reconstruction conjecture
- b. Cut vertex
- c. Travelling salesman problem
- d. Snake-in-the-box

ANSWER KEY

Chapter 1
1. b   2. d   3. d   4. b   5. d   6. d   7. c   8. b   9. b   10. d
11. d   12. d   13. d   14. d   15. d   16. d   17. d   18. d   19. d   20. c
21. d   22. d   23. d   24. d   25. d   26. c   27. d   28. c   29. d

Chapter 2
1. b   2. d   3. d   4. d   5. a   6. c   7. d   8. c   9. d   10. d
11. b   12. d   13. d   14. d   15. d   16. b   17. a   18. d   19. c   20. d
21. d   22. d   23. a   24. d   25. c   26. a   27. c   28. c   29. b   30. d
31. b   32. b   33. a   34. d   35. a   36. d   37. d   38. d   39. d   40. d
41. d   42. d   43. b   44. b   45. a   46. d   47. b   48. d   49. d   50. b
51. c   52. d   53. c   54. d   55. d   56. d   57. d   58. c

Chapter 3
1. d   2. c   3. a   4. d   5. c   6. a   7. d   8. a   9. d   10. d
11. d   12. c   13. c   14. a   15. b   16. a   17. a   18. c   19. a   20. d
21. d   22. a   23. d   24. b   25. d   26. d   27. d   28. d   29. d   30. d
31. d   32. d   33. a   34. c   35. a   36. d   37. d   38. c   39. a   40. d
41. d   42. a   43. d

Chapter 4
1. d   2. b   3. d   4. d   5. d   6. c   7. d   8. d   9. d   10. c
11. d   12. d   13. d   14. a   15. d   16. c   17. d   18. d   19. d   20. a
21. d   22. c   23. d   24. d   25. c   26. a   27. c   28. d   29. c   30. c
31. c   32. d   33. d   34. d   35. d   36. d   37. d   38. d   39. b   40. a
41. c   42. d

Chapter 5
1. d   2. d   3. d   4. b   5. d   6. d   7. a   8. d   9. d   10. d
11. a   12. d   13. b   14. c   15. a   16. b   17. c   18. c   19. d   20. d
21. b   22. a   23. d   24. d   25. a   26. c   27. a   28. d   29. a   30. b
31. a   32. b   33. d   34. d   35. c   36. a

Chapter 6
1. d   2. d   3. b   4. d   5. d   6. b   7. c   8. c   9. c   10. c
11. b   12. d   13. b   14. d   15. d   16. c   17. d   18. d   19. c   20. d
21. c   22. d   23. d   24. d   25. d   26. c   27. d   28. d   29. c   30. c
31. c   32. d   33. b   34. d   35. d   36. d   37. a   38. b   39. a

Chapter 7
1. d   2. c   3. c   4. d   5. d   6. b   7. c   8. c   9. d   10. d
11. d   12. c   13. b   14. d   15. c   16. d   17. b   18. b   19. d   20. d
21. d   22. d   23. d   24. d   25. c   26. d   27. d   28. d   29. a   30. a
31. d   32. d   33. a   34. a

Chapter 8

1. d	2. a	3. d	4. a	5. d	6. a	7. d	8. d	9. d	10. c
11. d	12. c	13. c	14. c	15. d	16. d	17. b	18. d	19. b	20. d
21. d	22. c	23. d	24. a	25. d	26. d	27. d	28. d	29. d	30. d
31. d	32. b	33. d	34. c	35. d					

Chapter 9

1. b	2. d	3. b	4. c	5. c	6. d	7. c	8. d	9. c	10. d
11. c	12. d	13. a	14. d	15. a	16. a	17. d	18. c	19. d	20. c
21. c	22. d	23. b	24. b	25. d	26. d	27. d	28. d	29. a	30. d
31. d	32. c	33. b	34. a	35. d	36. b	37. d	38. d	39. a	40. a
41. b	42. b	43. d	44. b	45. d	46. b	47. d	48. b	49. d	50. d
51. c	52. d	53. b	54. d	55. c	56. d	57. d	58. b	59. b	60. c
61. d	62. d	63. b							

Chapter 10

1. d	2. c	3. b	4. c	5. d	6. d	7. c	8. d	9. b	10. b
11. b	12. c	13. b	14. d	15. d	16. d	17. b	18. c	19. c	20. d
21. b	22. d	23. d	24. d	25. a	26. a	27. b	28. a	29. d	30. d
31. a	32. d	33. b	34. a	35. a	36. d	37. a	38. c	39. b	40. d
41. a	42. a	43. d	44. c	45. d	46. d	47. a			

Chapter 11

1. d	2. a	3. d	4. d	5. d	6. d	7. d	8. c	9. d	10. c
11. c	12. a	13. d	14. d	15. d	16. d	17. d	18. d	19. b	20. b
21. b	22. a	23. b	24. d	25. d	26. a	27. d	28. a	29. a	30. d
31. d	32. c								

Chapter 12

1. d	2. d	3. b	4. d	5. d	6. d	7. d	8. d	9. b	10. d
11. b	12. b	13. c	14. b	15. d	16. a	17. b	18. d	19. a	20. a
21. d	22. d	23. c	24. b	25. d	26. a	27. d	28. d	29. b	30. d
31. a	32. d	33. c	34. d	35. c	36. a	37. b	38. d	39. b	40. d
41. b	42. b	43. d	44. b	45. d	46. d	47. a	48. d	49. d	50. b
51. c	52. d	53. c	54. d	55. b	56. a	57. d	58. b	59. d	60. b
61. c	62. b	63. d	64. c	65. b	66. d	67. d	68. c	69. b	70. a
71. d	72. c	73. d	74. d	75. d	76. b	77. d	78. d	79. c	80. c
81. d	82. d	83. d	84. d	85. d	86. d	87. a	88. b	89. c	90. d
91. b	92. b	93. d	94. c	95. d	96. d	97. d	98. b	99. b	100. b
101. c	102. d	103. d	104. d	105. a					

ANSWER KEY

Chapter 13

1. d	2. d	3. d	4. d	5. c	6. c	7. d	8. d	9. a	10. c
11. d	12. c	13. b	14. d	15. d	16. d	17. d	18. d	19. d	20. d
21. b	22. c	23. d	24. c	25. d	26. a	27. d	28. d	29. a	30. c
31. b	32. d	33. d	34. d	35. d	36. d	37. d	38. d	39. d	40. d
41. d	42. d	43. d	44. c	45. b	46. c	47. d	48. d	49. d	50. d
51. c	52. d	53. d	54. d	55. d					

Chapter 14

1. d	2. d	3. b	4. a	5. d	6. b	7. b	8. d	9. d	10. c
11. c	12. d	13. d	14. c	15. b	16. d	17. a	18. d	19. d	20. c
21. d	22. c	23. d	24. d	25. c	26. d	27. b	28. d	29. d	30. d
31. d	32. d	33. b	34. d	35. d	36. d	37. d	38. a	39. a	40. d
41. c	42. c	43. c	44. b	45. c	46. b	47. d	48. c	49. d	50. d
51. b	52. d	53. d	54. c						

Chapter 15

1. d	2. d	3. c	4. d	5. a	6. d	7. a	8. d	9. d	10. c
11. d	12. a	13. d	14. d	15. d	16. b	17. d	18. a	19. a	20. d
21. a	22. b	23. c							

Chapter 16

1. d	2. d	3. b	4. c	5. c	6. d	7. d	8. b	9. d	10. d
11. d	12. d	13. a	14. c	15. b	16. d	17. b	18. c	19. d	20. b
21. b	22. c	23. d	24. d	25. d	26. b	27. d	28. d	29. d	30. d
31. b	32. d	33. c	34. b	35. d	36. a	37. d	38. a	39. d	40. a
41. a	42. c	43. a	44. d	45. c	46. d	47. c	48. b	49. a	50. a
51. d	52. a	53. b	54. d	55. d	56. b	57. d	58. d	59. b	60. c
61. d	62. b	63. a	64. c